Cults and Nonconventional Religious Groups

A Collection of Outstanding Dissertations and Monographs

Edited by
J. GORDON MELTON
Institute for the Study of American Religion

A GARLAND SERIES

MOONIES

A Psychological Analysis of the Unification Church

ROGER A. DEAN

GARLAND PUBLISHING, INC.
New York & London
1992

Library of Congress Cataloging-in-Publication Data

Dean, Roger Allen.
   Moonies : a psychological analysis of the Unification Church / Roger A.
Dean.
      p. cm. — (Cults and nonconventional religious groups) Originally
presented as the author's thesis (doctoral).
   Includes bibliographical references.
   ISBN 0-8153-0774-8 (alk. paper)
   1. Unification Church. 2. Cults—Psychology. I. Title. II. Series.
BX9750.S44D43 1992
289.9'6—dc20   92-20891
                                             CIP

Printed on acid-free, 250-year-life paper

MANUFACTURED IN THE UNITED STATES OF AMERICA

For Dorothy, of course.

TABLE OF CONTENTS

LIST OF APPENDICES

MOONIES

A Psychological Analysis of the Unification Church

CHAPTER I

PROBLEM

"The road of unselfishness is God's road
and you can reach him only by going in this
direction."

                    – Reverend Sun Myung Moon

In the past decade, America has witnessed
a startling increase in the number of young
people who have rejected the dominant values,
roles, and institutions of society to join
relatively authoritarian and totalistic
religious sects. Converts to these contemporary
religious movements acquire a new set of ideals
which promise to provide security, joy, and a
sense of purpose for their lives through the
elimination of ambiguity in their lifestyle. In
addition, members receive a new sense of
identity and intense feelings of interpersonal
warmth and friendship from fellow converts.
Membership, however, is not attained without
considerable sacrifice. Commitment often
involves strict regimentation to a demanding
schedule and unswerving loyalty to the group.
Further, converts are often encouraged to
withdraw from the usual worldly involvements and
are expected to lead lives of rigorous self-
sacrifice.

More importantly, the rejection of the
prevailing values of the culture generally

elicits strong sanctions toward the deviating
individual or group from members of normative
society. The majority of society unites against
what they feel to be a common threat to both the
morality and social order of the culture. By
collectively withholding its acceptance and
approval from any individual or group who
violates the prevailing norms, society
successfully manages to enforce its standards
and expectations on all but a small minority of
people. This study addresses a part of that
minority--individuals who somehow neutralize the
considerable weight of societal sanctions to
join a small, totalistic religious movement, the
Unification Church.

Current sociological theorists generally
accept the idea that young adults have acquired
certain dispositions from their culture, such as
attitudes, sentiments and needs which are
subject to particular expectations and supported
by sanctions from their culture (Wilson 1970).

Parsons (1951) noted that an individual's
conformity with a shared system of "value
oriented standards" is based on that
individual's concern with maximizing the
favorable responses he receives from others,
while concurrently striving to avoid any
negative sanctions from them. For most people,
Parsons observes, conformity to the dominant
value system is assured by a societal binding
process which results from the individual's
internalization and socialization into a common
value system. Thereby, internalization of a
society's values becomes a "need disposition" in
the individual's own personality structure.

Accepting this model of normative
behavior raises some intriguing questions in
relation to the Unification Church--most
notably:

In our society, where children grow up
generally adhering to some form of the Judeo-
Christian tradition, why do many young people
commit themselves to a religious movement so
different from their original value system?

4

Do members of the Unification Church have certain common characteristics which distinguish them from those who conform to societal norm?

Outside of the ideological rewards, are there specific underlying dynamics within the context of the group which attract potential members of the Unification Church?

Considering the strength of the sanctions enforced by members of society against the movement, how do individual cult members shield themselves against the psychological impact of these sanctions, so as to maintain a positive self image?

Because 'non conformist' activity becomes an important shaper of the perceived essential self, how do members of the Unification Church deflect the negative labels they frequently receive from society and also develop positive self images?

What is the role of Sun Myung Moon in the Unification Church? How much influence does he exert over the actual operation of the movement and the individual membership?

What is the process that the Church uses to bond members to such a deep commitment to a new set of ideals?

Moonies: A Critical Overview

When I began this study, I read voraciously the numerous accounts of cult existence written by either former members or established experts in the field of religious psychiatry. These reports presented a clear and consistent description of life within a modern day religious cult. Popular accounts characterized cult life as a cognitively and emotionally stultifying experience distinguished only by the frenetic pace of the group's religious activity. Members who populated these movements were portrayed as brainwashed, obedient servants, incapable of independent thought or reason. So overwhelming was the uniformity of these descriptions by reliable informants, that I accepted their reports as fact.

Dr. John Clark (1979), for example, a renowned authority on the American cult experience, identified an individual's rapid conversation into a "deviant" cult as a product of a massive dissociation brought about by the skillful manipulation of a naive or deceived subject" (p. 280). According to a 1980 unpublished paper by Dr. Clark, this dissociative state is characterized by several restrictions, most notably:

1) a narrowing and thinning down of the thought process (p. 13)

2) an inability to reconstruct the past in imagination (p. 9)

3) a suspension of critical judgement (p. 10)

4) difficulty expressing abstraction (p. 14)

Ted Patrick, an active deprogrammer of cult members echoed Dr. Clark's statements regarding the remarkable alteration that occurs in a convert's cognitive structure. "The most painful thing for a cult member to do," Mr. Patrick revealed at a Senate information meeting, "is to think." (p. 65) At the same meeting Rabbi Maurice Davis raised an even more ominous concern about life within a religious cult. "During the past five years I have helped rescue 128 young men and women...I tell you what I have done: I have peeled off the surface and entered an underworld of madness, and you have to see what I have seen to understand the horror of it all." (p. 77)

Consequently, it was with a sense of trepidation that I first approached the Moonies

on their home ground. Armed with a lifelong
attitude of religious irreverence, I felt
intellectually immune to their spiritual
solicitations. On an emotional level, however,
the Moonie cult, en masse, frightened me. I was
intimidated by the formidable mind control
techniques (reportedly mastered by each member)
which could transform well adjusted college
students into mindless zombies.

Despite my initial apprehension, I was
determined to remain open minded and investigate
the movement with objectivity. Throughout my
interaction with the cult I employed only one
basic assumption: that Moonies are rational
individuals who act in a manner consistent with
their view of the world. I believed a convert's
sudden and often radical departure from the
societally sanctioned value system could be
understood by examining that individual's total
life experience.

My early encounters with the church
membership (at their center in Detroit,
Michigan) shattered many of my original
stereotypes about the group. The Moonies I met
failed to conform to the robotized image
portrayed in popular books and scientific
journals. They appeared bright, funny, well
informed--people excited by both life and their
religion.

Where was the army of unthinking
automatons?

Where was the madness?

Where were the brainwashed servants
of Moon?

Over the next eight months I spent
considerable time interviewing, talking,
debating, and simply interacting with the
Moonies from the Detroit, Ann Arbor, and
Columbus, Ohio centers. I attended their
dinners, special events, and recruitment
workshop sessions. I came to understand the
Moonie perspective--to filter my reality through

their unique frame of reference. Behavior that
originally appeared irrational to me took on a
logical cast when examined from a convert's
perspective. Similarly, cult activities were
divested of their sinister overtones and
replaced by an empathetic awareness of their
motivations. To embrace intellectually an
unconventional viewpoint while maintaining a
very different perception of reality was an
exhilarating experience.

Experts and Former Members

        Initially, I was puzzled by the variance
between my own observations of the cult
phenomenon and those of both experts and former
members. Why did my experience differ so
dramatically from the previous studies and first
hand accounts of knowledgeable others?
Certainly the possibility exists that I was
unknowingly duped by the cult membership. If
this explanation were true, however, could a
group of programmed, unthinking Moonies provide
such reflective, lucid responses to my varied
questions? Their thoughtful statements,
interspersed throughout the body of this
dissertation, stand as direct testimony
affirming their intelligence and sensitivity.

        On the other hand, could the abundant
accounts of cult experts and former members be
in error while I alone hold the correct
interpretation? Taken at face value, this is a
seemingly preposterous supposition. However, I
will attempt to provide evidence that supports
this claim.

        Experts tend to lump together several
newly formed religious groups under the umbrella
of "cult". Thus, behavior and motivation
between widely disparate religious movements are
treated as virtually identical. By categorizing
cults according to overt similarities in their
recruitment practices, experts deny the
significance of each group's belief and value
system. Moonies rightfully chafe under the

8

comparison between themselves and other cults
such as Hare Krishna. Hare Krishna's
appearance, lifestyle, goals, interests, values,
motivation, and beliefs are completely unrelated
in any valid way with those of the Unification
Church. By overlooking fundamental differences
and labeling several cults as comparable,
experts disavow the internal complexity of the
Moonie organization. I believe any movement
such as the Unification Church can be understood
only in its totality.

Additionally, most experts' primary
contact with the Moonies results from clinical
or psychiatric treatment. Well adjusted
converts lack both the motivation and the money
to enter the mental health system as clients.
Consequently, former members comprise the
lion's share of psychiatric cult contacts.
These former members, often newly emerged from a
traumatic deprogramming experience and
struggling to regain their original societally
sanctioned perspective, present a disturbed
image of cult members to clinicians. As a
result, psychiatrists logically come to assume
that this select, emotionally unstable
population represents the functioning level of
the majority of Unification Church members.

Experts rarely have the opportunity to
observe cult members in their natural home
setting. Moonies generally view the psychiatric
community with suspicion--antagonists fully
entrenched within an opposing value system.
Misunderstanding and distrust on both sides
create conditions less than ideal for the mutual
acceptance of diverse perspectives.

On the other hand, I had the opportunity
to study the active cult membership within the
confines of their familiar home environment. My
ubiquitous presence eliminated any convert's
need for defensive posturing and allowed for
relaxed, informal relationships. Under the
circumstances, one should logically expect that
my observations of cult life should closely
parallel those of most former members. This,
however, did not prove to be the case.

Overlooking the realistic possibility of my own misinterpretation of the movement, there are several possible explanations for the disparities between our accounts.

First, the overwhelming majority of books and articles about life within the Unification Church are written by embittered former members. The public's desire for sensationalism has created a vast market for "cult atrocity stories". While financially lucrative (for both the author and the publisher) one sided reporting is obviously biased and precludes a balanced perspective of the entire Moonie experience.

Second, most former members have been exposed to a systematic anti-cult indoctrination program immediately after their departure from the group. Deprogramming, the most severe method, often involves forced removal from the cult, total confinement and aggressive value instruction until the reluctant convert admits his errors. The amount of coercion employed in the deprogramming efforts often exceeds that used by the Moonies to recruit the individual.

Third, former members are pressured by normative society to break completely their bonds to a deviant cult lifestyle. For a former member to waffle uncertainly about a cult related issue arouses uneasy suspicions in others that he remains partially under the control of the group. In most people's minds, cults are bad--therefore every aspect of cult life is bad. In order to be considered mentally stable (again) former members must become the most outspoken opponents of the group to which many devoted several years of their life.

Similarly, the inevitable maturity of both the movement and its membership may account for much of the observational inconsistencies that exist between former cult members and myself. It may be unrealistic to compare the Unification movement of five years ago (when many former members reported their experience) with the movement of today. The early cult was populated by inexperienced young people frantically attempting to establish a stable base for their foundling church. Lacking leadership training (or ability) many immature converts were nevertheless thrust into positions of authority within the group. Abuse of power became an all too common occurrence within the cult ranks.

Today, many of the excesses of the past have been modified or eliminated. Church officials are eager to present to the public a more conventional image of the cult. With its roots deep in conservative philosophy, the modern Unification Church seek respectability as eagerly as it once sought converts.

The elder statesmen of the movement, individuals who preserved their faith throughout the turbulent early years, have also matured, mellowed and taken on additional responsibilities. Those with tenacity and proven leadership talent have risen to levels of prominence within the cult. They have traded the rigors of fundraising for the security of executive level decision making, and strive to maintain their exalted positions. They too, are eager to see the movement solidify its position within the religious community and gain acceptance.

While the pursuit of new converts remains intense, Church strategy may be evolving a more effective method for increasing church membership without inviting public rancor (see "The Emphasis on Marriage and the Family" chapter 3).

Survival, be it that of a person, an organization or a religion, is based upon adaptation. The Unification Church's metamorphosis from cult status to accepted religion (in the United States) will depend entirely on the members' ability to outdistance the negative stereotypes firmly embedded in the American psyche.

Dissertation Format

In several ways, the following study does not conform to the typical dissertation format. The literature review, for example, was not consigned to its own unique section but rather interspersed throughout the body of the dissertation to provide clarity for the reader. Similarly, subject comments derived from numerous taped interviews were placed in strategic locations throughout the study to illuminate issues and explicate confusing concepts. The organization of the dissertation evolved naturally into six major topic headings:

1) The Unification Doctrine

2) Sun Myung Moon

3) The Attraction Process

4) Cult Recruitment

5) Typologies

6) Method

Located within the confines of each major topic heading are appropriately identified chapters. Each chapter addresses some facet of the overall topic. The topic headings and chapters have been arranged to acquaint the reader with essential information necessary to fully appreciate subsequent sections.

The Unification movement is made up of both male and female members. To eliminate the need for dual gender identification when referring generally to 'cult members' or 'recruits', the male pronoun will be employed exclusively in the body of this paper.

CHAPTER II

PHILOSOPHY

"I was thoroughly moved. Deep down in my heart it spoke the truth to me."
                                        - a 28 year old Moonie

"One full year after having joined—it was November 1974—I was standing in a snowy parking lot in Canton, Ohio. The wind was blowing through. It was dark-about 9 o'clock at night-and I realized that if I had known that this was going to happen—that I was going to be going through all this, I would never have joined. I had been led onto a path following the messiah—that was very painful realizing that."
                                        - a 24 year old former Moonie

If a new religious movement hopes to survive and flourish in the United States, it must introduce a compelling perspective which holds sizable appeal to at least some segment of the population. This philosophy must draw recruits with a galvanic intensity powerful enough to override their original religious orientation. Without the influx of eager new converts, a religion will stagnate, wither and eventually vanish.

The Unification doctrine, like that of many other religious groups provides adherents

with an elaborate philosophical and ideological
explanation of man's relationship to God and the
world. Prospective members are offered a
dynamic framework, replete with values, ideals
and orientations from which to view and
eventually penetrate the proposed meaning of
life.

More importantly, the doctrine promises
self fulfillment and satisfaction of physical
and psychological needs. These doctrinal
underpinnings invite youthful curiosity and
desire; emotions that may propel a recruit into
a lifestyle of exacting commitment to the
Moonies' unique perspective.

Background

"When I was sixteen years old an
extraordinary thing happened to me," recalled
Reverend Sun Myung Moon. "On a Korean hillside
on Easter morning in 1936 Jesus appeared to me,
telling me of God's desire to dwell in oneness
with man and to build His heavenly kingdom on
earth. Then Jesus called me for the mission of
being a messenger to give God's new revelation
to mankind. For me it was truly an awesome
moment."1

Over the next nine years Moon reported
receiving several additional revelations from
both Jesus and other prominent spirit world
figures. "I journeyed into the spirit world
many times," Moon disclosed. "In this truth I
could see the dawn of a glorious new
civilization. It was like a sunrise after a
long, dark night."2 From these revelations,
Moon developed a series of principles that
disciples believe provide crucial insights into
the relationship between God and mankind. These
revelations and principles later took written
form and are known today as the Divine
Principle.

The Divine Principle is the official
doctrine of the Unification Church. It presents

to the membership the correct understanding of
the Bible. The <u>Principle</u> does not center on the
conventional theological interpretation of the
Bible, rather, it contains in Dr. Thomas
Boslooper's words "a radical reconstruction of
an approach to the word of God."

Moonies believe that while the Bible
comprises God's teaching, every scriptural
passage is not meant to be interpreted
literally. The Bible, Moonies argue, is filled
with inconsistencies and contradictions when
read from a strict literal perspective. God's
intent can be better understood by recognizing
the obvious symbolic nature of numerous Biblical
passages. For true believers, the <u>Divine
Principle</u> holds the key to an accurate
reconstruction of the Bible's contents--a
reconstruction based on a divergence from the
traditional Christian acceptance of a literal
interpretation of the Bible to a more
symbolically oriented perspective.

Unification Church theology, however, is
not limited to unlocking the hidden meaning of
the Bible. The <u>Divine Principle</u> also explores
the nature of God and the goals of God's work
throughout human history. The <u>Principle</u> is
divided into three parts. The first part,
entitled "The Principle of Creation", explains
how God made the entire world of creation. Part
two, "The Fall of Man", describes man's fall
from grace, the origin of sin and the identity
of Satan. The third part, "The Principles of
Restoration", details the meaning and process of
salvation for man.

The <u>Divine Principle</u> as an Alternative
Perspective

A great deal of Unification Church
members' behavior can be understood when viewed
within the perspective of their belief system.
By accepting the Moonies' belief system as a
legitimate alternative perspective to the
traditional Christian approach, one can easily

15

discern the logic of their actions. Moonies are not acting out of a mindless, brainwashed condition. Rather, they are behaving in a rational manner consistent with their perspective of reality. For the most part, a Church member's reality is determined by the teachings contained in the Divine Principle. By studying the Principle one can understand why Moonies believe:

> the second coming of Christ will happen in their lifetime;
>
> each convert can attain total happiness;
>
> sex outside of marriage is a major sin;
>
> each member must dedicate himself/herself completely to the mission of the Church;
>
> Moon may be the new Messiah; and,
>
> Korea is the likely location for the second coming of Christ.

Divine Principle Outline Format

It should be noted that the following outline of the contents of the Divine Principle provided an extremely condensed and cursory summary of the original document. One cannot appreciate the complexity nor the subtlety conveyed in the original text from this brief review. I have borrowed literally and liberally from the Divine Principle and the Divine Principle Six Hour Lecture booklet provided by the Unification Church in the following account.

The Divine Principle

The Principle of Creation

According to the Principle, God exists in a special form, free of imperfection as the supreme ruler of the heavens. At some point in unrecorded time, God created both the universe and man. Like everything that God designs, man and his world resembled God in personality, nature, and purpose. God fashioned Adam and Eve, the first 'man' to be a very special creation. Designed in His image and nature they were formed to become God's children. Adam and Eve were to be the objects of God's love; as in all parent/child relationships they were expected to respond directly to the will and heart of their father. God originally conceived of their world as a perfect, joyful environment, free of sin and suffering. Adam and Eve were expected to enjoy lives of complete safety and happiness under the protective eye of their father--God. After life on earth, upon their physical death, Adam and Eve were to pass peacefully into the Spiritual Kingdom of Heaven. There, they would reside in eternal happiness under the perfect dominion of God's love.

While they were in a period of growth towards perfection, Unification theology holds, God gave Adam and Eve three blessings. The three blessings centered around God's ideal of love. The purpose of creation, God decreed, was for man eventually to fulfill these blessings.

God's first blessing was for Adam and Eve to grow to perfection so as to be one in heart, will, and action with God, having their bodies and minds united together in perfect harmony centering on God's love. The second blessing of God was for Adam and Eve to be united as husband and wife and to give birth to sinless children of God, thereby establishing a sinless family and ultimately a sinless world. God's third

17

blessing was for man to become lord of the
created world by establishing a loving dominion
of reciprocal give and take.

Had man achieved God's three blessings
Adam and Eve would have become the true mother
and father of all mankind and the world would
have become the Kingdom of Heaven on earth.
Before man could reach a state of perfection,
however, God decreed that Adam and Eve must
first experience a period of growth. God
decided that Adam and Eve could not simply be
perfected by His principle and power alone.
Rather, man had to fulfill a small but necessary
portion of responsibility for his own
perfection. Even though God deeply loved Adam
and Eve, he would not interfere with their
contribution towards their own perfection.

The Fall of Man

In the Garden of Eden, Adam and Eve lived
happily as brother and sister in complete
harmony with God's plan. They were blissfully
unaware of their intended future role as the
parents of all mankind. God had expected that
Adam and Eve would maintain this affectionate
sibling relationship until they matured into
perfection.

Before God had conceived of either man or
the physical world, however, He had created an
angelic world whose inhabitants acted as His
servants. The angels had lived in the company
of God's love and attention long before man
existed. When God created Adam and Eve as His
children, He considered them more precious than
His angels. To demonstrate His love, God
planned to entrust mankind with the privilege of
dominion over the whole of the created world--
which included the angels. When Lucifer, a
prominent Angel, discovered that God loved Adam
and Eve more than God loved Lucifer he became
extremely jealous. He desperately tried to
ingratiate himself with Adam and Eve to
supplement the love he was receiving from God.

18

Eve was growing daily in the abundance of God's
love (the ideal of all created beings); she
appeared extremely beautiful in Lucifer's eyes.
He was powerfully attracted to the God-like
qualities of Eve so he tempted her and seduced
her into an illicit sexual love. Thus, the
Moonies interpret the fruit of the Tree of
Knowledge of Good and Evil (which God had
forbidden man to taste) as simply a symbolic
representation of Eve's tragic fall from grace
through sex. This act of forbidden love, the
Divine Principle reveals, comprises man's
spiritual fall from grace.

        After the spiritual fall, Eve became
fearful as a result of the additional knowledge
given to her by her actions. She understood,
for the first time, that her true spouse was
meant to be Adam and not the angel. With this
new wisdom, Eve sought to return to Adam, in
part to correct her wrongdoing and in part to
alleviate the sensation of fear derived from her
fall. Consequently, she seduced Adam and this
second fallen act of love is known as the
physical fall. Through these acts, Adam and Eve
willfully turned away from God's purpose for
them, thereafter bringing themselves and the
entire human race into spiritual death.

        The root of human sin, The Divine
Principle relates, is not the accepted
interpretation of many simply picking and eating
a literal fruit. Rather, sin is the result of
Eve consummating an illicit love relationship
with a spiritual being (symbolized by the
serpent). This act established a fallen blood
lineage through which original sin is passed on
from one generation to the next.

        As a result of the Fall, Satan usurped
God's position as the father of mankind.
Consequently, all people are born in sin on both
a physical and spiritual level and have a sinful
propensity. Human beings, therefore, tend to
oppose God and His will. Lamentably, Moonies
believe that since Adam and Eve, mankind has
lived in ignorance of their original parentage
and pure nature.

The Principle of Restoration

Nevertheless, The Divine Principle
relates, God has not abandoned man or His ideal
of creation. While deeply saddened by the
course of human history, God is determined to
restore His lost children to Himself. Toward
this end God chose His son, Jesus Christ, to act
as Messiah to mankind. Jesus' purpose,
Unification theology states, was to come to
earth as the new Adam and establish himself as
the head of the human race. By replacing the
sinful parents, Jesus could establish a pure
family through whom mankind could be reborn in
God's family.

Before God would send His son, the
Messiah, however, he set certain steps in motion
to insure the success of the mission. God,
Moonies believe, chose the long suffering
Israelite race to establish a foundation which
would prepare the way for the coming Messiah.
Through numerous prophecies He foretold the
coming of the Messiah and warned the Israelites
to expect his coming. In order to complete the
preparation process God prepared a forerunner to
testify to the Messiah--John the Baptist. Thus,
the nation of Israel was passionately awaiting
the arrival of the Messiah.

Tragically, however, the much prepared
chosen people failed to recognize Jesus as the
true Messiah. The Son of God attempted to
reveal his Messianic identity to the Israelites
through words and deeds but they failed to
believe in him. He was branded a blasphemer and
ultimately crucified, thereby preventing his
building the Kingdom of God on earth. While
Jesus desperately wanted to reestablish the
ideal world of joy and happiness he was
unsuccessful in his mission.

Traditional Christian interpretation of
the Bible suggests that Jesus' death on the
cross was predestined and part of God's original
plan. The Divine Principle, however, holds that
it was a grievous mistake to crucify Jesus and
was the result of sheer ignorance on the part of
the people of Israel. Moonies believe that much
of the blame for this mistake must be placed on
the prophet John the Baptist who wrongly denied
that he was the second coming of Elijah.
Elijah, according to Israelist legend, was a
great Jewish prophet who lived more than nine
hundred years before the coming of Jesus. The
Jewish people were anxiously awaiting his return
because the Old Testament clearly foretold that
Elijah would precede the Messiah and point the
correct way.

When Jesus' disciples went out among the
people of Israel testifying to Jesus, the Jewish
masses remained unconvinced. Where, they asked,
was the prophet Elijah? Jesus rightfully
indicated that the popular Jewish prophet John
the Baptist was the new Elijah that the people
had been long awaiting. John, however, denied
his role as Elijah, failing the Israelites in
his responsibility to acknowledge Jesus as the
true savior.

Consequently, the Divine Principle
posits, the entire nation of Israel (including
Jesus' own disciples) could not believe in and
receive Jesus. Therefore, God had to give
Jesus' body away (the crucifixion) to Satan as
the condition of indemnity to save all of
mankind who had fallen onto the side of the
Devil.

God nevertheless used his power to
resurrect Jesus' spirit (an area Satan was
powerless to invade) making possible spiritual
salvation for those who are reborn through him.
After his resurrection, Jesus remained on earth
for forty days. He gathered together his
scattered disciples and instructed them to
follow him even at the cost of their lives.
Upon this foundation Jesus was elevated to the
position of spiritual Messiah. Consequently,

Moonies believe that the spiritual realm into
which Jesus was resurrected is secure from
Satan's invasion. They are convinced that Jesus
has decreed spiritual sanctuary for those reborn
in him.

In spite of this refuge, however, man is
still subject to the Devil's corrupting
influence through his physical body. God was
forced to ransom His son's body to Satan as
indemnity for man's sins. Jesus' crucifixion
and subsequent resurrection resulted in the
spiritual salvation of mankind. Nevertheless,
physical salvation still remains to be achieved.
Thus, Moonies fervently hold that the complete
restoration of the Kingdom of God on earth
awaits the Second Coming of Christ. To
eliminate original sin and be completely free
from it in both body and spirit, the Lord must
come again to fulfill God's purpose of creation.

The Second Coming

The Divine Principle states that the
Second Coming of Christ will occur in our age,
an age very similar to that of the First Advent.
Christ will come as he did before, as a human
man. He will establish a family through
marriage to his bride (a human woman). Together
they will become the true parents of all
mankind. The Divine Principle stresses the
humanity of Jesus while recognizing his
relationship as the son of God. His
resurrection, Unification theology maintains, is
a spiritual rather than a physical resurrection.
Moonies posit it is a grave error for man to
expect a god-figure unlike Jesus as the second
Messiah.

Recognition and acceptance of the true
parents (The Second Coming of Christ) is an
essential step toward salvation. By obeying the
true parents and following them, original sin
will be eliminated and believers will eventually
become perfect.

22

Because of the importance of this second mission God could not just send the new Messiah to the world without extensive preparation for his eventual acceptance. When the people of Israel failed to accomplish their mission as the central nation of dispensation, church theology states, God began to form the Second Israel-- multi-racial Christianity. Moonies believe Christianity was established by God to supplant the Israelite nation and prepare the foundation for the second coming of the Messiah. From this Christian group, God has selected some dependable individuals upon whom he can rely to obey His every command. These hand-picked individuals have been instructed by God's emissary (Reverend Moon) to form groups that are physically and spiritually separate from the evil that characterizes the rest of the world. Followers must be dedicated solely to the mission of building a foundation for the arrival of the coming Messiah.

Providential Time-Identity

To understand when and where the Second Coming of Christ will occur one must study a Divine Principle concept known as Providential Time-Identity. Moonies believe in a unique cyclical view of human history. They see God's hand in the design of all life events. History is perceived as a series of parallel time periods loosely controlled by God. When individuals (or whole nations) fail to accomplish God's intended mission, He is forced to start anew. Consequently, when periods of pre-Christian history are compared with periods of post-Christian history, striking similarities in time, place, and human activity are evident to converts. The reason why startling cyclical patterns in history exist, Moonies argue, is due to God's desire to return man to his natural state of goodness. When the first Israel did not complete its responsibilities and failed to believe in the Messiah, God had no choice but to prolong his providence of restoration.

23

Therefore, after the coming of Jesus until the time of the Second coming, the providence of restoration was repeated.

Providential Time-Identity divides history into two blocks, each containing six comparable time periods. One block, "The History of the First Israel" began with Jacob and ended with the birth of Jesus. This period lasted approximately 1,930 years. The second block, "Christianity", began with Jesus and ended with the Messiah--a period again totaling 1,930 years.

Obviously, the year 1930 was not the year in which the Second Coming of the Messiah was to occur since that time has already passed. The Divine Principle states, however, that the Lord of the Second Advent, like Jesus, must go through a preparation period in private life and a period of public ministry to prepare the foundation to realize the purpose of the Messiah's coming. Therefore, in view of the providence of restoration, Moonies are convinced that this is now the time of preparation for the Lord's second appearance.

The location of the Second Coming of Christ has never been revealed, although Jesus clearly indicated that he would not return in the land of Israel where he had been killed. From a Time-Identity viewpoint, Moonies suggest that the nation of Korea is the most likely location to receive the Second Coming. Korea, they point out, has several important Time-Identity similarities to the First Israel: notably "a national history of suffering and misery, a tradition of filial piety and loyalty, and a strong inclination toward religious life". In addition, Korea is frequently mentioned in revelations about world salvation by spiritually gifted clergy and laymen.

By accepting the Unification Church's Time-Identity perspective, one could logically assume that the Second Messiah is a Korean-born holy man whose birthdate roughly coincides with

the calendar year 1930. Interestingly, the
Reverend Sun Myung Moon's life matches these
criteria.

CHAPTER III

ANALYSIS OF DOCTRINE

"It was so logical, but I still wouldn't
give it an acknowledgement. I was still Mr.
Cool on the outside but on the inside bells were
ringing and stuff and I said, 'Wow! How do they
know all that? I thought I was the only one who
knew all that.'"

- a 28 year old Moonie

"Once you are exposed to this ideology
you start to reframe reality according to this
ideology...that's one big difference between you
and the world. You see yourself in a totally
different light. You see yourself as looking
like a human being but you're really God's
representative...what you want is the goodness
of all mankind whereas what people out here (non
Moonies) want is basically their own happiness.
They are out for their own selfish benefit. So
you really hold yourself in a much different
esteem--and you hold others differently. You
just start to refilter everything through--
everything."

- a 26 year old former Moonie

Few young people are truly interested in
seriously exploring a new religion. To a large
extent, religious values are deeply embedded
within an individual's personality structure and

highly resistant to drastic alterations in
content. What then, is the magnetic appeal of
the Divine Principle, that tens of thousands of
young people willingly dedicate their lives to
promoting its message? Certainly the cult's
recruitment style, conversion techniques and the
personality characteristics of the converts
(topics discussed in subsequent chapters)
contribute to—and cannot be separated from, the
answer to this complex question. Nevertheless,
an effective recruitment and conversion program
would be an exercise in futility if the doctrine
was implausible. To attract and hold followers,
a religious group must develop a doctrine that
is credible (on a cognitive or emotional level)
to some segment of the population. It must
offer to the convert an advantage that
conventional religions fail to provide.

By analyzing the underlying themes of the
Divine Principle and its presentation format,
some explanations emerge for its startling
acceptance among broad segments of young people.

The Devil

The ideological framework of the Church
is grounded in a simple adversarial relationship
between the forces of good and evil. The lines
of combat are unmistakenly drawn—the antagonist
clearly pictured. By strategically placing the
Devil on one side and itself on the other, the
Unification Church accomplishes several notable
psychological functions simultaneously. First,
by employing the devil as their central
adversary, the cult closely identifies itself
with the roots of most accepted religious
philosophies. The Divine Principle recreated
the familiar and reassuring struggle between
good and evil. On its most basic level,
recruits are not obliged to develop an entirely
new symbolic orientation to grasp the armature
of the group's perspective. The familiar is
less frightening. More importantly however, the
similarity of the Devil concept to the recruit's
pre-established orientation lends credibility to

28

the cult doctrine. A.D. Nock (1961) observed this principle in his study on religious conversation. "The originality of a prophet is commonly in his ability to fuse into a white heat, combustible material which is there, to express and to appear to meet the half-formed prayers of some, at least, of his contemporaries. (pp. 9-10)

Second, the Devil provides a durable antagonist to unite the membership in a common cause. Satan is emblematic, evil incarnate, making him an unsympathetic foil for the Church's accusations. Converts naturally presume that if they are warring upon forces of pure evil, it stands to reason that their diametrically contrasting perspective must be pure righteousness.

Third, the Devil offers a symbolic but nevertheless acceptable explanation for all personal, group and world problems. On an individual level members can expiate personal responsibility for offensive behavior by projecting their blame outward, onto an agent (Satan) external to themselves. "The Devil made me do it" takes on a literal meaning to Moonies, far in excess of the comic intent that popularized the phrase.

On a larger scale, dissonance can be effectively eliminated in every conceivable dilemma by merely recognizing Satan's presence in an activity, person or situation that runs counter to the movement's goals. The Devil is graphically portrayed in Moonie literature as a malevolent, powerful antagonist with a singular purpose--to crush the Unification Church and eradicate its principles. The failure of outsiders to comprehend the wisdom of the Divine Principle, Moonies assume, results from Satan's pervasive influence over non-members rather than faulty logic among the converts.

Security

The Divine Principle provides many
youthful members with an uncompromisingly rigid
philosophic interpretation of life which brings
order to their confused world. The doctrine,
recruits are informed, presents a set of truths-
-irrefutable and absolute. As a result,
ambiguity and complication fall away magically
from the recruit's life once he wholeheartedly
embraces the cult's ideology. A sense of the
absolute correctness of their mission is perhaps
the most striking characteristic of any
fledgling Moonie.

Recruits distressed by the complex and
often conflicting standards prevalent in modern
society can discover sanctuary in the womblike
certainty of the Church's totalitarian ideology.
One female, former Moonie described the
confidence she received from living in her
regimented environment.

> "It gave me an assurance of knowing what
> was going on in the world – of what I
> could expect and what my role was in the
> world. I knew exactly, no questions. I
> mean everything from tying my shoes to
> how I wore my hair. I knew what the
> right way and the wrong way was. And
> there was a right way and wrong way to do
> everything."

Increased Self-esteem

A dramatic rise in a convert's self-
concept frequently accompanies his membership in
the Church. Several reasons for this soaring
self-regard can be linked indirectly to the
cult's ideological approach.

Moonies confer considerable status upon
one another for wisely perceiving the true path
to Godliness. Acceptance into the movement,

converts come to believe, implies a certain
spiritual superiority. Members look upon
themselves as the "spiritual elite" divinely
pre-destined to alter the course of human
history.

The solution to all problems is within
the collective grasp of mankind, Moonies trust.
Mass acceptance of the Divine Principle will
result in Satan's overthrow - eradicating human
suffering and misery forever. By espousing a
philosophy that purports to provide universal
clarification for man's most perplexing
problems, members are able to invest one another
with a heightened sense of self-importance. For
youthful members generally weak in qualities
society rewards, (education, experience, etc.)
identification with a profound system of thought
can be an exhilarating experience.

The Divine Principle invests the
membership with a universal perspective and an
exciting sense of purpose. Feelings of
frustration and confusion are transformed into
sincere asceticism and devotion to principles of
a higher order. Petty concerns of daily
survival pale in significance to global issues
of world salvation. Moonies toil cheerfully
under the harshest of circumstances, not because
they are brainwashed automatons, but rather
because they sense the significance of their
contribution to the larger mission.

Escalating a person's self-regard can
have a striking impact on that person's ability
to be objective toward the person rewarding him.
Hitler (1939) recognized this, "when the
disappointed are given a sense of importance
they will swallow every suggestion with the
utmost docility". (p. 241)

Suffering

Suffering - paying indemnity for past and
present offenses against God is a central
hallmark of the Unification theology. Members

fast for days, deny themselves sleep or invent
myriad other personalized torments to repay God
for sins committed by themselves and mankind.
On the face of it, a policy requiring individual
anguish should drive all but the most fanatic
converts back to the halls of conventional
churches. This, however, does not prove to be
the case for most members. The Divine Principle
imparts awesome nobility to the concept of
suffering. As a result, suffering has become a
crucial exercise in a Moonie's spiritual
development. Self-denial is considered virtuous
and thus, is its own reward. Moonies take pride
in their self-discipline, ascetic attitude
toward material possessions and arduous lifestyle. Their willingness to suffer bravely
stands as a distinct counterpoint to the
hedonistic, Satanically influenced attitudes of
American Society. Further, suffering purifies
the spirit, purges buried guilt and lends deep
purpose to each member's religious commitment.
The personal appeal of suffering for a cause was
expressed by one male former member:

> "Because I was kind of a prim, abstemious
> sort of person the idea of doing
> without - punishing myself - that wasn't
> really foreign to me. The notion that if
> you are going to accomplish great things
> you've got to strive greatly. That made
> sense to me. It felt right".

Frankl (1959) suggested that suffering is an
important way for a person to discover meaning
in life. "In accepting this challenge to suffer
bravely" Frankl noted, "life has meaning up to
the last moments." (p. 206)

Far from being a negative feature of the
cult, suffering may act as a catalyst to amplify
the convert's initial enthusiasm for the
movement.

Trouble Free Future

A world liberated from poverty, disease
and unhappiness is the ambition and optimistic
expectation of every new Moonie convert.
Nirvana, the Divine Principle holds, can be
attained in the membership's lifetime. The
siren call of a worldly paradise lures both
idealists and malcontents alike. Their
acceptance of the Moonie doctrine springs from
an eager, often urgent need to hear an uplifting
message that allays their fears and imparts
unbounded hope for the future.

The Moonie perspective provides a
refreshing contrast to the fire and brimstone
approach of other major religions. Rather than
being threatened into submission by the prospect
of impending disaster, the convert is soothed
and reassured by the Unification doctrine. The
Divine Principle's interpretation of the "Last
Days" presents an excellent example of their
elevating message of global perfection. Rather
than adopting the traditionally held explanation
of the physical destruction of the world or the
banishment of all sinners; the Divine Principle
posits that the 'Last Days' signify an end to
pain and disbelief among man. God will reign
victorious on the Last Days by removing the
sinful sovereignty of the Devil forever. What
is destroyed, the Principle relates, is not the
literal earth itself but sin, death and the
false control of Satan, all of which are
symbolized (in the Bible) by the earth.

By accepting the Moonie explanation, the
emotions of fear and apprehension about the
future (and one's personal destiny) are
transformed into feelings of hope and
reassurance.

Presentation of the Divine Principle

The manner in which the Divine Principle
is transmitted to potential recruits represents

33

the most crucial phase of the conversion
process. Unification ideology, members realize,
must be presented in both an interesting and
convincing fashion to attract new followers.
Consequently, Moonie recruitment centers are
staffed with competent personnel who wisely
coordinate every facet of the instruction
program. Church trainers (those members who
actually conduct seminars and teach the Divine
Principle to recruits) are articulate
Unification seminary graduates. In addition to
mastering Unification theology, trainers are
well versed in the ideological and philosophical
framework of several major religions. Further,
Unification trainers are veterans of numerous
identical seminars (both as a trainer and
observer) where their delivery and techniques
have been honed to perfection. To the
uninitiated recruit, listening to his first
series of lectures, the trainers' knowledge of
the Bible and religious philosophy may appear
awesome.

        The Divine Principle, trainers realize,
presents a radical philosophic departure from
the recruits' original religious orientation.
For the most part, recruits entering their first
seminar bring with them a conventional
perspective of religion that is highly resistant
to change. The trainers' demanding task is to
convince the skeptical potential recruits of the
authenticity of the Unification Church's
theological orientation. To achieve this goal,
trainers must accomplish two essential
objectives:

        1) They must create an atmosphere which
        casts doubt upon the recruits' original
        religious orientation, causing him to
        question his belief system.

        2) They must present a more credible and
        meaningful alternative theoretical
        perspective.

        The first series of lectures is designed
by the trainer(s) to stimulate recruits to
examine and question their religious belief

system. By simply convincing recruits to acknowledge the logic of interpreting certain Biblical passages as symbolic, the trainer accomplishes a vital step in the conversion process. Providing scriptural evidence to support their perspective, trainers assault recruits with frequent examples of contradictions and inconsistencies in the traditional literal interpretation of the Bible. Young Oan Kims' Moonie centered analysis of the Bible, entitled <u>Unification Theology</u>, makes reference to several different types of evidence which suggest that the Scriptures are not infallible: most notably 1) Obvious contradictions such as Exodus 37:1-9 which states that Bezalel made the ark of the covenant while Deut. 10:1-5 claims that Moses made it. 2) Biblical contradictions to known truth including the assumption that all diseases are caused by demonic possession and the suggestion that the earth is immovable, and 3) frequent evidences of legend-making such as hero tales in Judges which closely resemble those of the Greeks.

Once doubt and confusion have been firmly implanted in potential recruits regarding the correct interpretation of the Bible, the trainer merely reformulates a more logical version--The Divine Principle. Trainers skillfully outline a consistent step by step explanation of the Unification theological approach for recruits. When Unification beliefs diverge from or contradict the more traditional Christian perspective, trainers clearly document their interpretation through scriptural quotation or reliance upon a common sense analysis of events. Why, recruits are asked, would Adam and Eve be banished from the garden of Eden for simply eating the apple? Why would Jesus call John the Baptist the greatest of men and then refer to him as less than the least in the Kingdom of God? (Luke 7:28) If Jesus knew and accepted his predestined crucifixion, why did he cry out in despair that God had forsaken him? (Mark 15:34)

Through the Unification interpretation, (a more symbolic understanding of events) these apparent contradictions are made logical for the confused recruits.

For many individuals, the most impressive aspect of the Unification theology is Moon's cyclical reformation of human history. This complex conceptual orientation confers a sense of intellectual legitimacy on the Unification perspective by suggesting to young recruits that the movement evolved from a scholarly background. Such a formidable and logical religious orientation, many recruits come to believe, cannot be dismissed easily as just another crazy cult.

While the bulk of the seminar presentations rest with the trainer(s) he has considerable assistance from fellow members. Several Moonies sit through each lecture acting as role models for the new recruits. Often surrounding the recruit on all four sides, converts accentuate important lecture points by vigorously nodding their heads in agreement or making subtle verbal exclamations. Members encourage recruits to take copious notes on the lecture material as they themselves do. Writing the Unification theology down serves not only to recreate the familiar trusting atmosphere of earlier school days; it also increases the recruits' comprehension of the material and enhances the likelihood of its acceptance. For most people, the written word has power; it cannot be easily disregarded. If I don't believe this philosophy, a conforming recruit may reason, then why am I writing it down? What many recruits may not realize is the subtle but pervasive pressure exerted by the membership to ensure that everyone conforms to the group's expectations. Failure to take notes implies a rude lack of interest or non-cooperation on the part of the recruit. To be fully accepted and rewarded by the seminar participants each recruit must comply with the established structure of the lectures. The formal teacher-student relationship thrusts the recruit into a

submissive inferior role, where he is socialized
through rewards to attach great significance to
the Divine Principle. As a result, a formerly
skeptical recruit, without understanding why,
may discover himself accepting unquestioningly
controversial beliefs of the Unification Church.

CHAPTER IV

MARRIAGE AND FAMILY

"Person to person witnessing is not the best way, in the long run, to bring in new members. In the initial stages it's good."

                              - a 32 year old Moonie

"That's the real test--the second generation. Whether the philosophy and the religion can provide a meaningful tradition for the family. I think that if it does the community will hold together beyond the next generation--after Reverend Moon dies and our children grow up. A lot of people who joined in the middle 70's are six or seven years older and most of them are engaged or married now. They have to start thinking about long term considerations."

                          - the same 32 year old Moonie

In the waning moments of the year 1980, over sixteen hundred church members from 127 different countries waited with feverish expectation inside the Grand Ballroom of the former New Yorker Hotel. Outside, thousands of their fellow members congregated in eager anticipation, awaiting the results of the most dramatic ritual in the Unification Church. The cause of the members' excitement stemmed from the Church's unique marital matching ceremony presided over by Reverend Moon. Unification converts from the world over assembled in New York City for one purpose: to allow Reverend Moon to select their future mate. Since 1960, Reverend Moon has matched and married more than 3,000 couples, a distinction that has merited him several entries in the Guinness Book of World Records. Few couples will have ever seen or met their future spouse prior to their being matched for marriage. For the members, the ceremony represents a giant leap of faith. For the Church, the matching ritual represents a decisive step in the solidification of the movement.

That most members enthusiastically yield their right to personal choice of their mate is neither an act of irrationality nor the result of some insidious form of brainwashing. Moonies' accepting attitude towards the mate matching ritual can be logically understood by examining their motives through the perspective of the Unification Church belief system. Unification theology places considerable emphasis on the sanctity of marriage and the need for a strong family structure. The family, Moonies believe, is the cornerstone of their religious faith. As such, the family must be considered sacrosanct and be protected and nurtured. Moonies believe that biological attraction (the primary basis for romantic love) is a poor foundation for choosing a future spouse. Rather, it is much more reasonable, they maintain, to rely upon the divinely inspired mate selection process employed by Reverend Moon. "God", one Moonie acknowledged, "knows who will make a better wife for me that I do."

Arranged marriages have certain advantages for the individual members. Moonies eschew the current dating scene as a time consuming and troublesome method of seeking a lifelong partner. With the Unification mate selection process, Moonies can concentrate their full attention on their important life mission without being distracted by romantic decisions. Fear of rejection is also avoided by complying

40

with the arranged marriage concept. Members
believe that mates are chosen by Moon for
important inner qualities not always readily
apparent at first meeting. For shy, disfigured,
or homely members, arranged marriages may be
attractively perceived as their only opportunity
for connubial happiness. In addition, Reverend
Moon's control over his followers' marriage
partners has considerable long range benefits
for the Unification Church. Perhaps the
persistence of this controversial nuptial
ceremony owes as much to its organizational
utility to the movement as it does to
ideological principle.

Most single people in America spend
considerable time and energy attempting
(directly or indirectly) to attract members of
the opposite sex. Through the ritual of dating,
eligible youth are accorded an acceptable
societal outlet to evaluate either the marital
potential of their dating partners or reaffirm
their own appeal for future prospects. For the
army of young, single converts that make up the
bulk of the Unification Church membership in
America, mate selection and marriage are also
important concerns. While members are dedicated
to the successful completion of their religious
mission they are not unaware of the biological
and emotional forces that govern all human
nature. Moonies, like everyone else, want the
security, warmth, and companionship of a
successful marital relationship. However, when
personal considerations override religious
obligations, Moon realized, the foundling
Unification movement suffers. Arranged
marriages provide the Church hierarchy with an
excellent organizational solution to offset
their young members' natural inclination to
spend valuable time and energy seeking a mate.
It discourages romantic liaisons among the
membership by creating a mind set that dampens
personal initiative in the mate selection
process. Under the more common romantic
perspective, it would be unrealistic to thrust
young male and female members into a communal
living environment and expect them to maintain
an attitude of sibling warmth toward one

another. Under the arranged marriage
perspective, however, Moonies confidently await
their divinely chosen mate. All others, no
matter how personally attractive to the convert,
are considered unattainable and improper to
pursue on a romantic level.

Arranged marriages also ensure that
Moonies marry other Moonies--a fact of
immeasurable importance to the continuation of
the Unification movement. The religion-based
family unit is the foundation upon which the
Church hopes to survive and prosper. The
movement's emphasis on family unity can be
viewed as an essential requirement for future
growth. Church officials recognize that the
offspring of a dedicated Moonie couple will
likely be inculcated with the religious values
and belief system of their parents. By marrying
committed followers and encouraging them to
raise large families, the Church painlessly
expands geometrically with each successive
generation. The movement's ban on birth control
and its outspoken denunciation of divorce among
Church members can be understood as a strategy
to preserve the Church's religious ideals
through its members' children. With a firm base
of enthusiastic parents instilling the Church
theology into countless offspring, the movement
need not resort to the individual recruitment
methods of its recent past. Expansion will be a
natural outgrowth of the movement's family
pattern.

SUN MYUNG MOON

CHAPTER V

REVEREND MOON

"He moves his arms around, stomps on the floor, pounds the podium, does these spins and turns, he whispers then he shouts. I thought this guy is either totally crazy or the messiah. I mean, no one else would do this. This man has courage to speak this way."

- a 25 year old former Moonie

"Such a man, who begins to cry whenever he prays, there has to be something important about that man--different about that man."

- a 24 year old Moonie

The Unification Church's phenomenal rise in stature, influence, and membership in the United States can be directly attributed to the leadership ability of one man--Sun Myung Moon. Born into a struggling North Korean family, Moon today dwells in regal splendor in America, reigning autocratically over a multi-million dollar religious empire. Moon's climb from unknown ascetic to world prominence rests upon his galvanic appeal to youthful admirers, resulting from his accomplishing three basic procedures.

1) Recognizing and defining the collective discontent of a variety of socially and psychologically disparate youth in American.

2) Formulating a compelling doctrine based upon the principle of divine authority which embodied many of the personal aspirations and fantasies of youth.

3) Developing a charismatic leadership style that elevated his doctrine out of obscurity and into a public conception that could be accepted on a cognitive or emotional level by youth.

Collective Discontent

As a struggling young holy man in search of an army of followers to build the foundation for his church, Moon wisely concentrated his efforts on those most likely to alter their viewpoint--youth. "Conversion," William James observed in his classic book Varieties of Religious Experience, "occurs most among those beset by a sense of incompleteness and imperfection." (p.195) At no other time in an individual's life cycle is the potential for dissent with the prevailing norms so compelling as during youth. As Erikson (1968) noted, adolescence and young adulthood is a stage in human development characterized by an identity crisis which contributes to the individual's feelings of confusion, isolation, and dissatisfaction during this period.

The source of the discontent may be as varied as the individuals experiencing the crisis but it is generally conceived around the growing awareness of the discrepancy between the youth's inflated expectations and the reality of his situation.

By recognizing, crystallizing and responding to the universal discontent of the

youth, Moon forged a powerful bond of
identification between himself and an otherwise
diverse group of people. He wisely expressed
this sense of dissatisfaction in general
universal and transcendental terms which the
young could identify with on a personal level
while still retaining appeal to a broad based
constituency.

"The adolescent," Erikson stated, "looks
most fervently for men and ideas in whose
services it would seem worthwhile to prove
himself trustworthy." (p.129) To his
idealistic young supporters, the intent of
Reverend Moon's message is clear. Do not
suppress the awareness of your discontent, nor
revise your expectations; rather, join me in a
mutually shared vision of a perfect society
where your world will match your expectations.

To the romantically inclined, Moon offers
a heroic vision of equality, harmony, and
victory over injustice. Suffering and
persecution, youthful admirers come to believe,
are natural and inevitable outgrowths of their
courageous efforts to alter the world.

To the alienated, Moon provides a
meaningful sense of purpose and direction in
their lives. Boredom evaporates as the young
person commits himself to the ideals of the
Church and Reverend Moon's mission to save
mankind. By constructing and communicating his
utopian idea, Moon clearly offers broad sections
of discontented young people a new and concrete
option for the construction of their lives.

"I wasn't looking for the temporary
happiness that most people are looking
for," observed one male Moonie. "I was
looking for a chance for eternal
happiness--serving--helping other people,
making other people happy. Reverend Moon
taught me how to achieve these goals."

Formulating the Doctrine

In formulating the Divine Principle, Moon relied on two central themes to appeal to discontented youth.

First, he understood that the doctrinal perspective must counterbalance youths' dread of an unpromising future by presenting a sweeping vision of optimism about the destiny of the world. Thus, the Divine Principle contains a mystical reinterpretation of the history of Christianity which elevates into prominence sections of the Bible which emphasize hope, faith, and salvation. The Principle's fundamental message announces the arrival of a second messiah: a Christ figure who will vanquish Satan and restore mankind to its rightful state of eternal happiness. To accomplish this aim, converts believe, God has called upon special human messengers (Moonies) to spread the news of the messiah's arrival.

Second, Moon applied the important Machiavellian principle that power is vested in those who claim divine authority. While Moon falls short of actually proclaiming himself the messiah, he repeatedly emphasizes his role as God's chief representative on earth. He legitimizes this claim of rightful authority through his self described visionary association with Jesus and other saints.

Developing Charismatic Leadership

Moon understood that in order for his doctrine to be heard and accepted, he must somehow emerge as a leader capable of arousing and maintaining a devoted following. Toward this end, he struggled relentlessly to cultivate an image of competence and vigor.

Moon recognized very early that leadership of a religious cult is a relational phenomenon, involving the interaction of both the leader and his followers. It is not what the leader is, but how he is perceived by his followers that determines his right to command. The cult members' collective consensus of Moon's leadership confirms his power and transforms him into a total authority. "The distinguishing criterion of authority," Blau (1956) notes, "is the structural constraints rooted in the collective acceptance of subordinates rather than the instruments of power or influence wielded by the authority figure which enforce compliance to his directions." (p.22) If one accepts this interpretation of authority, then Moon's meteoric rise to prominence as a powerful cult leader can best be understood within the framework of Max Weber's concept of charismatic authority.

Weber (1974) identifies charismatic authority as authority which rests on the "devotion to the specific sanctity, heroism or exemplary character of an individual person and on the normative pattern or order revealed." (p.328) He defines charisma as "a certain quality of an individual personality by which he is set apart and treated as endowed with supernatural, superhuman or at the least specifically exceptional powers or qualities." (p.358)

Anecdotes from Moon's colorful early life provide the cornerstone for the three qualities upon which his charismatic appeal is built: spiritual deification, extraordinary bravery, and almost superhuman strength.

Church legend tells how Moon, as a young man, was wrongfully imprisoned in a communist labor camp for preaching religion in the streets of Pyangyan. Conditions in the camp were bleak yet Moon never succumbed to his oppressors. Tortured and starved, he continued to preach God's word while sharing his meager food allotment with other prisoners. Upon his liberation in 1950 by U.N. forces, Moon

courageously led a small group of disciples over
the mountainous terrain to religious freedom in
South Korea. During this arduous journey, Moon
is said to have saved a fellow prisoner with a
broken leg by carrying the man on his bicycle
six hundred miles through the mountains to
Pusan.

Divine Authority

       Much of Moon's early success in
mobilizing support for his church can be traced
back to his followers' belief in the divine
nature of his leadership skills. Prevailing
against such overwhelming circumstances lend
considerable credibility to his religious
message and self described association with
Jesus. By effectively projecting an image of
himself as a God-inspired leader, Moon not only
attracted early converts but he also laid claim
to spiritual authority over them. "It is
charismatic leadership," Weber observed, "that
legitimates and sustains charismatic authority."

       As the Unification movement developed so
did the level of sophistication employed by Moon
to intensify his charismatic appeal. The Divine
Principle, formerly preached orally, took a
fixed form, was written down and frequently
elaborated upon by Moon. Early converts were
instructed (as they are today) to dedicate their
lives to the ideals and mission proclaimed by
Moon to be God's will for mankind. As God's
chosen spokesman Moon fashioned a self image
that assures him power and collective
idealization from admiring adherents. If one
accepts the beliefs of the Divine Principle,
then recognition of its originator's role and
level of spiritual purity cannot be logically
questioned.

       Missionaries were trained to convey the
message of the Divine Principle (and not
unimportantly Moon's carefully sculpted image as
God's spokesman) to cities throughout Europe,
Japan, and the United States. Elaborate

communication networks were developed to
disseminate Moon's orders, plans, and
philosophic concerns to eager missionaries
throughout the world.

In order to gain wide acceptance from the
world community, Moon realized that he must
expand his appeal beyond his small band of
faithful devotees. He understood that in
religion, money and converts represent power--
power that can easily be garnered into
legitimacy and respectability.

Toward this end, Moon decided in 1971 to
relocate the headquarters of the Unification
Church from Korea to the United States. By
establishing a firm foothold in the richest and
most powerful nation on earth Moon hoped to gain
reflected prominence and stature for both his
church and himself.

A relative unknown outside of his own
country and Japan in the early 1970's, Moon
thrust himself energetically into an extended
campaign to convince Americans of the sincerity
of his mission. A spellbinding orator (even
though he speaks little English) he crisscrossed
the country during the 1974-1975 Day of Hope
Lecture Tour speaking to thunderingly
enthusiastic audiences in all fifty states. A
master of manipulation, Moon often turned a
dissenting voice to his advantage. A former
member recounts one such situation:

> "This guy jumped up in the balcony and
> shouted down right in the middle of his
> (Moon's) talk, 'Man, I have been
> listening to you for over a half hour' -
> the whole audience stopped - 'You have
> been talking for a half hour, lover boy,
> about love and peace. If you're so big
> on love, why don't you go back to South
> Korea and talk some love into good old
> Park Chun Lee? Your own country is in
> shambles.' Of course the Moonies came up
> from behind him, grabbed him by both arms
> and escorted him out the door. Then Moon
> said, 'I want to thank this man for
> coming tonight. He has made tonight such

an interesting and rich night.' People
just gobbled it up. They thought it was
great."

Expanding the Movement

While outwardly professing an egalitarian
philosophy, Moon actually cultivated a complex
hierarchical status system within the movement--
a system which provided prestige and rewards for
those in executive positions. Advancement
within the cult was (and still is) based not
only on loyalty to Moon and his doctrine but
importantly on the members' ability to bring
large quantities of money or converts into the
organization. Moon justifies this materialistic
stance by contending that a spiritually pure
member would inevitably deliver positive results
to the Church. Those who fail, Moon reasons,
must have an internal spiritual problem which
affects adversely their external achievements.
Thus, the most direct method for zealous
converts to prove to the Church hierarchy (and
to themselves) that they are growing spiritually
is by bringing ever increasing amounts of money
or members into the movement.

In the cult's quest for converts and
money little is left to chance. Moon and his
top advisors systematically partitioned the
United States into regions where sophisticated
teams of seasoned fund raisers periodically
journey in search of money or converts. Known
as Mobile Fund Raising Teams (M.F.T.), these
specialized squads have but one central aim: to
amass vast sums of money for the Unification
coffers. To accomplish this goal, team members
rely on the sale of such items as candles and
flowers or make direct appeals for donations.
With competition for advancement within the cult
ranks intense, fund raisers are ever alert for
receptive potential recruits along their
travels. Success in attracting new recruits
often leads to a less rigorous position in a
Church center away from the grueling pace of the
fund raising teams.

Fund raising is considered by many
Moonies to be the most demanding assignment a
member can be appointed to. Mobile fund raisers
can expect to be away from their base center for
extended periods, living and sleeping in crowded
Church vans purchased specifically for these
activities. Motivation to succeed is high--
advancement out of full time fund raising.

In order to assist individual initiative
even further, Moon has sponsored activities
designed to generate a competitive atmosphere
among the membership, as one former Moonie and
frequent M.F.T. leader recalled:

"He (Moon) just got one contest after
another for fund raisers. There are 20
day contests and 40 day contests where he
pits member against member, team against
team, region against region--all in
heavenly competition."

The obvious effect of these frequent
contests was to escalate the level of individual
motivation among his following, all of whom
hungered for personal recognition from Moon. Of
course an inevitable side effect of this
increased effort was the increased funds which
entered the Church's coffers.

Power Through Association

A technique used to stunning effect by
Moon to gain and solidify his charismatic appeal
was to present an image of power and prominence
by associating with those who had it. Moon was
quick to recognize the value of acquired
prestige--reflected public approval resulting
from affiliations with popular figures in
America. An expert at public relations
techniques, he masterminded an elaborate program
to acquire political influence through
associations with famous and powerful American
leaders. Six distinct, but interlocking,
approaches were employed to provide Moon contact

with or influence over important political or
religious dignitaries.

First, Moon engaged an internationally
recognized dance troupe, known as the "Little
Angels", as a key instrument in his initial
design to win access to important world
dignitaries. The "Little Angels" acted as
Moon's personal forerunners, opening doors that
would have otherwise remained closed to the
aspiring religious figure.

"With their record set up in other
countries," Moon related in 1973, "the
Little Angels can be invited to the
premier's mansion or the palaces of kings
and queens and will be known to the
people of these nations." (Master
Speaks, January 30, 1973)

As he predicted, the "Little Angels"
concerts furnished the ideal medium for Moon to
mingle with dignitaries and have pictures taken.
Subsequently, many of these photos were
reprinted and found their way into Unification
organizational literature, where he was
deceptively portrayed as a man with numerous
influential "friends".

Second, Moon used his longtime
connections with prominent Korean political
figures to arrange meetings with well known
American dignitaries. Again, photographs were
taken to document Moon's association with the
famous and were later reprinted in Church
literature to magnify his image of power.
Eisenhower, Humphrey, John Kennedy, and Nixon
were but a few of the high ranking dignitaries
photographed with Moon whose pictures later
graced a Unification publication.

Third, Moon launched a campaign among his
followers to solicit endorsements from political
or church leaders at every level of government
of church organizations. In a 1974 speech, Moon
emphasized the significance of the numerous
endorsements he received nationwide during the
then-recent Day of Hope Tour.

"As you know they have sent many
telegrams and congratulatory messages.
In doing this they are lending us the
entire weight of their names...This will
lift our movement up to the pinnacle."
(Master Speaks. March 24, 1974)

Later in the same speech Moon went on to
elaborate on the utility of garnering written
support from prominent individuals.

"When you go get the proclamations in
your various cities and you must meet the
Mayors, it is easy because your
foundation has been laid. All you have
to do is show other proclamations, other
letters, and say what other people have
done to honor Father." (Master Speaks.
March 24, 1974)

Fourth, a U.S. House subcommittee
investigation into activities of the Unification
Church determined that Moon had created a number
of small, highly specialized public relations
teams in the Washington area. Comprised almost
solely of young female Moonies, each team
endeavored to cultivate friendships among
Congressmen and members of their staff. Once
these strictly platonic relationships were
firmly grounded in affection each woman worked
tirelessly promoting the Church and dispelling
any unflattering impressions of Reverend Moon.

Fifth, Moon is not unaware of the awesome
power he wields among his devotees. He has on
occasion used his capacity to mobilize instantly
hundreds of disciplined followers to promote
rallies or demonstrations which prove
politically advantageous to his movement.
Moonies, 1,200 strong, for example, turned the
1973 national Christmas tree lighting ceremony
into a well rehearsed show of strength in
support of President Nixon.

Sixth, each year in the United States,
Moon sponsors a prestigious international
conference on science to which he lends both his
name and his financial support. The

54

International Conference on the Unity of the
Sciences (I.C.U.S.) provides a forum for
scholars from fifty countries (an all expense
paid trip) to discuss critical scientific and
philosophic issues facing mankind. Unification
critics charge that Moon's underlying motivation
for sponsoring the conference has little to do
with his interest in championing scientific
enterprise; rather, they maintain it is a
transparent attempt to win worldwide academic
respectability. Conference advocates, on the
other hand, cite the considerable service Moon
provides to the scientific community by
providing a timely and unbiased opportunity for
the most outstanding minds in science to gather
and discuss urgent world issues.

Future Goals

        Sun Myung Moon's driving ambition to
achieve a level of stature and influence
worldwide is well known to anyone who hears him
speak publicly or privately. His vision of a
future world order dominated by a theocracy and
governed under the direction of God is wholly
consistent with his philosophic ideals. Who
better to run the world than God? In this
"unified civilization" the separation of church
and state would be abolished as unnecessary, as
would all languages except Korean. Moon, of
course, would naturally occupy a central role of
authority in this new world order as the
following passage from a 1974 Master Speaks
speech suggests:

        "The time will come without my seeking it
        that my words will almost serve as law.
        If I ask a certain thing it will be done.
        If I don't want something, it will not be
        done. If I recommend a certain
        ambassador for a certain country and then
        visit that country and that ambassador's
        office, he will greet me with the red
        carpet treatment." (Master Speaks, March
        24, 1974)

For Moon and his followers, a worldwide theocracy has none of the sinister implications those opposing him would have the public believe. In unity there is peace and prosperity for all people--those born in Bombay as well as those born in Boston. Under the single banner of the Unification Church, philosophic and moral differences will be eradicated forever. War will cease to be a viable solution as mankind melds together in a singular purpose. This idea of a universal brotherhood is eloquently expressed by one idealistic Moonie:

> "I see something happening on T.V.--on the other side of the world (people) starving. I turn off the T.V. and go back and eat my steak. Don't bother me, I'm an American! Well we are all a part--we are all connected. So when one part is hurting we are all hurting. Mankind is connected that way. (We need) more universal thinking, more universal consciousness."

Moon's idealized vision of world theocracy in the future is not without obstacles in the present. Money and followers, in unprecedented numbers, are necessary to forge his dream into a reality. In a 1974 Master Speaks address, Moon contemplates the path to his goal:

> "The world is really our stage. We are going to be the ones who restore and bring hope to every corner of the world. The money is there and I will earn that money. And you will become soldiers, trained soldiers." (Master Speaks, January 31, 1974)

The quotation above provides a telling description of Moon's envisioned future role. It is obvious that his egalitarian ideas do not extend to his relationship with his followers. Moon sees himself as a powerful leader of the future world and he works unflaggingly to promote strategies which will achieve his aim both outside and inside his organization

Once a charismatic relationship has
developed, Weber observed, the leader is
relatively immune to any further challenge to
his power as long as that relationship prevails.
To maintain the delicate balance of this
relationship and avoid the prospect of a
significant organizational challenge to his
leadership role from within, Moon appears to
have taken several preventative steps.

Frequent member relocation, enforced
celibacy and arranged marriages all function as
safeguards to forestall the formation of
dominant in-groups. Familiarity breeds intimacy
and trust--emotions counterproductive to both
the movement and Moon. Long term relationships
may lead to confusion over issues of personal
responsibility among members. Should a Church
directive oppose the best interest of an
intimate sub-group, members would be forced to
choose between their loyalty to the movement and
their friendship with their peers. In the
Unification Church allegiance must be sworn to
only one master: Sun Myung Moon.

Trusting relationships developed over a
long time period would also increase the
likelihood of unguarded disclosures among
intimate members. Shared discontent could have
unsettling ramifications on the frail
charismatic base upon which Moon's power
resides. Collective dissatisfaction, voiced
openly, could shake the very foundation of the
movement.

Through repeated relocations of
underlings Moon effectively eliminates the
potential for powerful in-groups forming at the
lower echelons of the movement. Moon, however,
must also keep a watchful eye on top advisors
and members of his administrative staff. Church
officials, working daily with Moon, may prove
less susceptible to the Unification image
machinery that surrounds him. They may view
Moon as vulnerable and recognize the precarious

underpinnings of his dominance over Church
devotees. As a result, ambitious Church leaders
may at some point wish to wrestle some measure
of control away from Moon's autocratic grip and
win some power for themselves. To avoid this
prospect, Moon retains control over every major
policy decision. All lines of authority
converge in Moon's office and orders that
emanate from him flow through a complex
hierarchical administrative system to individual
members. By concentrating the power for all
important decisions in his own hands, Moon
eliminates any prospect of a crucial policy
statement being formulated by Church staff which
would run contrary to his best interests.

Advancement to a position of importance
within the movement is based not only on ability
but importantly on ardent personal allegiance to
Reverend Moon. Finding fault with Church
procedures almost assures a rebellious convert a
lowly station within the cult hierarchy. Open
questioning brings resounding sanctions from
other members and casts overwhelming suspicion
upon the offending convert's current spiritual
status. Spiritual status, as every aspiring
Moonie realizes, is a barometer employed by the
Church leadership to determine an individual's
potential for promotion. Moonies quickly learn
that total compliance leads to positions of
status and comfort, while dissention (no matter
how constructive) offers nothing but rejection
and criticism. Fearing a loss of approval,
members are exceedingly wary of discussing
Church issues in a manner their peers may
construe as critical. As a result personal
concerns go unvoiced in the membership's rush to
present only an optimistic perspective. By
basing promotions on the singleminded devotion
to the Unification perspective, Moon effectively
chokes off any overt opposition to his
leadership.

On a very basic level, questioning a
decision or motive of Rev. Moon produces
tremendous dissonance among the cult membership.
To doubt Moon is to doubt the very armature of
the movement. If Reverend Moon is wrong about

58

this issue, a follower may reason, then perhaps
he is wrong about other things as well. To a
convert who has relinquished most of the
comforts and financial advantages of normative
society for grueling months of dawn to dusk
proselytizing for Moon, this questioning process
may prove unnerving.

While Moon can suppress the outward
expression of doubt or dissatisfaction among his
devotees, he cannot control their personal
thoughts. Almost every Moonie has at one point
questioned his faith, confronted some shattered
illusions, or simply wearied of the taxing daily
schedule. Wisely, new members are groomed early
on to expect and even anticipate this reaction
as another outgrowth of Satan's struggle to
undermine the movement. Nevertheless,
frightened or discouraged adherents are far more
likely to share their discontent with fellow
members than are those eager for promotion. The
contagious nature of fear or doubt in a close
knit group could evoke a rippling effect among
the wavering converts causing mass desertion
from the cult. To counteract this tendency,
Moonies are frequently admonished to behave in a
happy, effusive manner, particularly when they
are experiencing serious doubts about their
involvement in the movement. As a result of
this strategy, a faltering convert will not only
avoid transmitting a powerful negative message
to his peers, but he may also feel better by
pretending to be happy. Social psychological
research has supported the notion that people
often gain control over their emotions by
consciously altering their behavior. As early
as 1884, psychologist William James noted that
"If we wish to conquer undesirable emotional
tendencies in ourselves, we must assiduously and
in the first instance cold bloodedly, go through
the outward motions of those contrary
dispositions we prefer to cultivate."

THE ATTRACTION PROCESS

CHAPTER VI

ATTRACTION

"I felt part of a wonderful movement,
filled with beautiful people, a beautiful
leader, a view that will change the world. We
were going to do it--we can do it. You can't
match that, as artificial as that is, as crazy
as that is, and even though it just shatters on
the rocks because it can't work - it's not
realistic - those few minutes is an experience
that few people ever experience in their entire
lives."

- a 24 year old former Moonie

"My goal was to hit every church they
had. Go to every church because I had a feeling
that one of them had to be right."

- a 22 year old Moonie

Attraction to a group can be defined as
all the resultant driving forces acting on an
individual to gain, maintain or avoid membership
in a group. The Unification Church is in a
growth stage and the group devotes considerable
time and energy to the process of attracting and
converting new members. Like any growing
business enterprise, the Unification Church has
a product (philosophy, lifestyle, etc.) which
its members must attractively package and
promote to the American consumer in order to

reap a profit of new recruits. To accomplish its goals of increased membership, the group must overcome some initial obstacles.

First, the cult must convince potential recruits that its product (philosophy) is worthy of examination and consideration as an alternative to the philosophical structure to which they currently adhere. This is an extremely difficult task as religious values are deeply embedded within the individual's personality structure and are highly resistant to conventional reformation.

Second, the group must neutralize the negative impressions held by the majority of the American public toward the group and establish a sense of confidence in its place. An essential factor is the development of an image of trustworthiness and respectability.

Third, the group must promote its philosophy to a population with a broad diversity of values, goals, needs, interests, and backgrounds.

Finally, the group needs to excite intense emotions within potential recruits in order to motivate them to devote the extensive time and energy necessary to effect a conversion.

In order to overcome the above noted obstacles, the Unification Church must carry out four rudimentary but essential procedures:

1) designate an appropriate target population;

2) provide recruiting personnel with ready access to that target population;

3) develop successful methods for gaining favorable attention from the target group and;

4) provide incentives for the potential recruit to maintain his interest in continued and prolonged involvement with the group.

CHAPTER VII

TARGET POPULATION

"I wanted to be free — free of hassles; free of emotional problems; free of relationships."

— a 26 year old Moonie

"I got really caught up in the Camelot thing. The new frontier — torches to be passed — the Peace Corps. Things like that."

— a 26 year old former Moonie

The Unification Church focuses the majority of its recruiting and proselytizing efforts on youth. Potential members are frequently sought among college students who come from white, middle class, or affluent backgrounds. In a survey of 237 Unification members in California, Galanter (et. al. 1979) discovered that 89% of the respondents were white, 91% were unmarried and 47% indicated that they had attended school on at least a half time basis during the six month period prior to their joining the sect.

To understand why young people may be particularly vulnerable to the ministrations of the cult one must look to some of the psychological, social, and emotional experiences occurring in youth. This can best be understood by examining the stages of normative development that generally predominate in individuals during this period.

Identity Struggle

Erikson (1968) has postulated that the search for identity is the critical crisis and major preoccupation of youth. For Erikson, identity is "the capacity to see oneself as having continuity and sameness". (p.50)

Most young people experience identity confusion at some point in their development. This crisis arises out of the search for a reliable and consistent framework on which to hang the development and crystallization of their newly emerging identity. To construct a coherent identity, each individual must develop his own unique synthesis from the models, ideals, and identifications available to him in society. "In its search for that combination of freedom and discipline, of adventure and tradition, which suits its state, Erikson (1958) observed, youth may exploit (and be exploited by) the most varied devotions. Subjecting itself to hardships and discipline, it may seek sanctioned opportunities for spatial dispersion, follow wandering apprenticeships, heed the call of frontiers, man the outposts of new nations, fight (almost) anybody's holy wars". (p.42)

If, however, the youth fails to find consistent models and ideals to which he can satisfactorily relate, he will experience an identity crisis. It should be noted that the term "identity crisis", as used in this context, refers to Erikson's (1968) definition of the concept and does not necessarily have any long term negative implications for the described individual. It simply refers to "a necessary turning point, a crucial moment, when development must move one way or another, marshaling resources of growth, recovery and further differentiation". (p.16) Normative identity crises are a natural pattern of growth among young people.

A by-product of the identity crisis is a condition known as identity diffusion. This condition is characterized by feelings of anxiety, confusion, disorientation, and frequently a deep sense of isolation. The youth may find social relationships with others, be they friendships, cooperative endeavors, or sexual encounters, unsatisfying or difficult to maintain. The outer world is often viewed by the identity diffused youth as frightening, chaotic, and incomprehensible.

When an individual finds himself overwhelmed by worry and bewilderment about himself and his world he may begin to question the accepted values and social framework which no longer satisfy his needs. Eager to free himself from the psychological and social discomforts in his life the youth may seek alternative standards or ideals, identifications or lifestyles to achieve relief. But as Erikson (1968) warned "...any experimentation with identity images means to play with the inner fire of emotions and drives and to risk the outer danger of ending up in a social pocket from which there is no return". (p.158)

In addition to the likelihood of some form of identity diffusion, youth, by its very nature, has several characteristics which might increase young people's attraction to the philosophy and ideals of the Unification Church.

Idealism

For many individuals, youth is a time of great ideological receptivity, which results in a desire to improve the world. Social problems and their solutions seem to stand out with clarity. The injustice and lack of concern for one's fellow man greatly disturbs these idealistic young people. "It just seems", one Moonie passionately said, "that the whole world around me was caught up in turmoil and I kept wondering why? Why? Why? Aren't we all brothers?" For the idealistic youth, movements like the Unification Church hold great appeal. The cult offers each convert an opportunity to help rectify inequalities prevalent in society. Unification Church literature emphasizes each member's role in designing a better world. Prejudice, poverty, drug abuse, sexual license, and the threat of nuclear destruction are but a few of the social problems Moonies believe they will eradicate in their lifetime.

For many of these young people, conventional churches lack the ideological fervor capable of inspiring their commitment. They view their religion in active terms and want a movement into which they can channel their expansive ideological energy. "Truth", one Moonie eloquently expressed, "only has value if it is lived".

Being involved in a collective idealistic movement can be very exciting. To be young and committed to a high moral cause has considerable romantic appeal. A former Moonie described the emotional atmosphere of the group: "There was a great intensity about the whole thing. Being involved in this project where everybody had their energy so focused upon it. It was really a sense of being involved in a big thing. You got really caught up in it--in the sense that you were making a difference in the world and you were really doing something important".

Intellectual Curiosity

More than any other age group, adolescents are spiritually and intellectually open to new ideas. They are eager to experience new challenges that improve both themselves and the world. Many youths, however, lack the sophistication and intellectual experience to evaluate critically the emotional sales pitch of

a movement. With a weakly established set of
ideals and values, the young person may be
unable cognitively to differentiate the subtle
but important distinctions between opposing
norms. A movement, like the Unification Church
which presents a clear, uncompromising vision of
a better world appeals to many young people.
"Youth," Coe (1900) observed in his analysis of
adolescence has "a passion for absolute truth
indubitable certainty, perfect righteousness
about all this is most real." (pp 54-55)
Young people's naive inclination to categorize
groups or situations in a strict black or white
manner is due at least partially to American
childrearing techniques. Role models such as
parents, teachers, and coaches often instill in
children the concept that there is a simple
right or wrong distinction in every situation.
Similarly, television heroes and villains are
portrayed in a rigid good/bad stereotype which
ignores the complexities of human nature.
Consequently the young must learn through
experience that a person, idea, or philosophy
must be judged on its total merits rather than
initial impression.

Recruiters take advantage of naive young
people's simplistic perspective and desire for
idealistic experiences. One former Moonie
recounted a major reason for her eventual
conversion into the Unification Church as
follows:

> "They kind of guilt tripped me. How can
> a self respecting individual who cares
> about the world not give it a try...if
> you think there is one chance in a
> million that it will work, how can you
> not try? If there are certain things you
> don't agree with--just go along with
> those things you do agree with...you
> never understand everything anyway...and
> I prided myself on being an open minded
> person willing to learn new things."

Disillusionment

        Caught in a difficult transition between
childhood and adult maturity, many young people
experience prolonged periods of dissatisfaction
with their lives. This sense of discontent is a
major factor in their exploration of alternative
norms and lifestyles.

        College students in particular may
experience strong feelings of disillusionment
with their environment. Away from home for the
first time, students must make massive
adjustments in their lives in order to remain
psychologically stable. New students, for
example, frequently miss the emotional support,
status, and security that they had come to rely
on from their parents and community. Freud
(1936) noted that it is separation or the fear
of separation that triggers much of the anxiety
in humans. Feeling lonely and alienated in a
strange new environment, some students may
desperately, and indiscriminately, seek out a
new support system to stave off the fear of
isolation.

        Similarly, students who were high
achievers in high school may find the
competition of the university's academic and
social standards extremely rigorous. They may
fear (realistically or otherwise) that they
cannot perform adequately. Beck and Young
(1978) estimates that perhaps 78% of all
students enrolled in American colleges suffer
for an extended period from symptoms of
depression. The anxiety created by making
important life decisions which have major
implications for the future (such as career
choice) can further escalate the unhappy
students' feeling of discontent. Thus, one can
understand how a student who is approached by an
exceptionally friendly, sincere, and tranquil
cult member could become intrigued. Perceiving
the recruiter's outward sense of calm to be
almost the opposite of the turmoil they feel
within themselves, the students want to find out

what the recruiter knows that they don't. When the recruiter extends a casual dinner invitation to meet and talk with like minded others, the student may be eager to accept.

The social framework of modern society also contributes to restless college students' exploration of alternative norms and lifestyles. A major result of advanced civilization has been the extension of the term of social adolescence which delays the time at which many young people assume adult roles and responsibilities. As society increases in complexity, educational demands on the young increase and require an additional investment of years of training for work. Erikson (1968) refers to this societally sanctioned intermediary period as a kind of "psychological moratorium" (p.143) in human development, often characterized by "a combination of prolonged immaturity and provoked precocity." (p.156)

This moratorium has several important implications for the social development of many college students.

First, students generally remain financially dependent upon their parents and must retain an adolescent attitude of subordination in their relationship with them.

Second, increased educational demands generally delay the age of marriage. This tends either to lengthen the period of sexual postponement or create the need for an alternative to sex within marriage.

Third, the moratorium results in the achievement of educational goals taking priority over the commitment to a career work.

Fourth, students are afforded the time and opportunity to experiment with a variety of roles and identity models.

Discontent among the young however is not limited to college students. Restless young people from all backgrounds and educational levels travel daily from city to city, continent to continent, in search of something to believe in. One former Moonie described a typical exodus.

> "I realized that I had been to the mountain top and I wasn't seeing any clearer. Somehow I thought if I just got to the Rocky Mountains, or just got to see the ocean, that somehow I'd be more interesting--have it better together somehow."

Another former member recalled his emotional state in more pragmatic terms: "I was in the space where most people who get converted are. They are at loose ends. They are looking for something; they don't know what it is, and they are in California and they are trying to find it."

Moonies recognize that disillusioned, rebellious, and disoriented youths are the most susceptible to new leadership and conversion. A young person who openly questions societal norms provides valuable information to the recruiters which suggests that he is an individual dissatisfied with the current societal framework or his position within it. The recruiter will attempt to use this sense of discontent to the cult's advantage by presenting an attractive alternative to the potential recruit's current lifestyle: the Unification Church.

Guitar cases, duffle bags and backpacks alert recruiters to the potential rootlessness of their carriers, making them prime targets for a "spontaneous" introduction. Recruiters frequently seek out prospects in bus stations, historical landmark sites, and city parks where large numbers of wandering or aimless youths are likely to congregate. The lure of instant friendship in a strange city, the potential for some interesting philosophical discussions on interesting topics with peers or the simple offer of a free meal often provides the initial impetus for involvement with the cult.

A devastating personal loss may also increase a young person's susceptibility to the Unification Church. Crises such as the death of a family member, a failed romance or a severe financial setback may propel some youths to seek consolation within a religious framework. Initially the individual will turn to his traditional religious roots for comfort. Failure to find relief, however, may lead the young person through a dizzying succession of alternative religious experimentation. Moonies, Galanter (1979) noted, were frequently involved in other non-traditional religious organizations prior to their membership in the Unification Church. A traumatic event involving personal loss creates an ideal atmosphere for a religious conversion. The young person, stunned by his loss, is at an emotional crossroads. Desperately struggling to reformulate his life, he may question his values and reasons for existence. Often, he will experience deep feelings of guilt over causing his misfortune. This vulnerable perspective can lead to a period of high emotional intensity as one male Moonie, forced into bankruptcy, recalled.

> "I had an experience then with Christ. Realizing all the things that I saw was wrong with the world and how people treat each other, I realized that I too was just as responsible. I too had done my share of ripping people off and not being completely honest. I realized that I too had been hurting God. So I repented. I mean, I repented very deeply through tears...I was crying profusely in my big house - that the bank was going to be taking soon. All my friends had disappeared. And I said 'Why is all this happening?'"

Later in the same day he described his first encounter with a female Moonie in a downtown city.

"Like the spirit said--Look at my
children. So I started really looking at
people now, closely. And I saw that
people were either looking down at their
feet or they were staring forward
blankly. No one was talking to each
other...I started crying. People
unhappy--actually I was unhappy--actually
God was unhappy, but I hadn't made the
connection. All these people, walking
down the street turned to a stream of mud
before my eyes. It was very spiritual;
it was like a river of mud. And I saw
one person, shining brightly, walking
down the street. It looked like she was
walking on air."

CHAPTER VIII

STEREOTYPED IMAGES

"The very day that I met the church I
never drank and never smoked again. Never had
any desire to. The reason I drank was because
something in me was empty. I was missing
something--I was unfulfilled."

- a 24 year old female Moonie

"Self indoctrination is an important part
of the cult phenomenon. It's not just the
group. Moonies indoctrinate themselves to
believe what the group believes."

- a 25 year old former Moonie

The image of the Unification Church and
the Moonies in the public's mind has been shaped
primarily by those strongly opposed to the
group. Former members and parents of children
involved in the Unification Church have written
numerous exposes about life within the cult.
The proliferation of these articles and books
has led to a widespread negative impression of
the group in America. For the most part,
Moonies are genuinely puzzled by the furor that
has grown up around both them and their
movement. They chafe under the public's
conception of converts being brainwashed robots
or deluded zealots. They view themselves as
courageous missionaries in a hostile land: a
band of spiritual elites enthusiastically

battling the forces of evil on earth. That society fails to recognize the legitimacy of their movement causes considerable consternation to the membership. A type of black humor arising out of the bitterness and irony of their position in society is revealed in their conversational anecdotes. One member, for example, described a recent door-to-door sales campaign from a cult member's perspective. "Many people do awful things to you in the name of Christianity. It's O.K. to persecute a Moonie. It's O.K. to be rude; I'm just some zombie at their door. They say, 'I'm a Christian. Get the hell off my porch.'"

In emotion laden issues, such as cult membership, the prior perspective of the observer often determines whether a believer is judged as good or bad. Undeniably, normative society with its powerful media machinery, has placed its stamp of disapproval on the Unification Church. The immense power of society to assess the merits of any outgroup has not escaped the observation of most Moonies. Taking a mock societal perspective one member observed, "If you were in my church and you were doing those things, you would be a great American--a great Christian person. But you're involved with that group and no matter how much good you do, it's a front."

Moonies cite hair style as an interesting example of society's effort to associate negative connotations with the cult. "Suddenly," one Moonie wryly noted, "parents were complaining that their son or daughter was disgustingly clean cut." Similarly, parents who visited their offspring at Unification Church facilities reported being upset by the cleanliness of the quarters and the seemingly All-American existence of the membership. "There was something very sterile about the atmosphere there," one mother remarked. "It was very simple, very clean, very nice. Ordinarily a mother should like that...but it was so alien, so foreign to her (the daughter). Her room at home and her room at the dorm was unbelievable-- but it was like everybody else's room." Concern

over dramatic change in their children's
behavior (good or bad) is understandable from a
parent's point of view. Would the parents,
however, be equally concerned over the same
behavior if their son or daughter were serving
in the military or attending an ivy league
school? Depending on your perspective,
identical behavior can be viewed quite
differently. What one person perceives as
brainwashing, another person looks upon as a
dedicated commitment to an idealistic religious
movement. What one person sees as endless days
of proselytizing, another perceives as an
ascetic sacrifice to a compatible religious
lifestyle. Unquestioning obedience can be seen
as robotization or total faith and loyalty to an
inspiring leader.

Moonies' perception of their movement
closely approximates William James' definition
of religion at its best. In his classic book
The Varieties of Religious Experience James
(1929) defines the best as 1) "A feeling of
being in a wider life than that of the world's
selfish little interests; and a conviction not
merely intellectual of the existence of an Ideal
Power." 2) "A sense of the friendly continuity
of the ideal power with our own life, and a
willing self surrender of its control." 3) "An
immense elation and freedom as the outlines of
the confining selfhood melt down" and 4) "A
shifting of the emotional center towards loving,
and harmonious affections, toward 'yes, yes' and
away from 'no' where the claims of the non ego
are concerned." (p.266)

Society approaches the concept of
religious commitment from a very different frame
of reference. Most people would agree that
religion is an important if not essential
variable in their life. It is not, however, an
all consuming passion whose importance dwarfs
every other aspect of life. Consequently, it is
difficult for people to accept the Moonies'
total dedication to an unfamiliar set of
religious principles. "They don't understand
your heart, or your circumstances, or your
motivation," observed one Moonie. "You're just

77

crazy. Who serves God this much--sent off in some little place. Who serves God that you're out fundraising in the rain?"

Society's perception of the cult members' behavior has inevitably led to the formation of a number of stereotypes. While there appears to be some truth to each statement, under close scrutiny these stereotypes do not hold up.

Stereotype 1.) Moonies are all alike. If you have met one you have met them all.

Moonies are as diverse in personality, temperament, interests, goals, and perspectives as any group of individuals who are seriously linked together by a common purpose. Some members are serious and intellectual, while others are exuberant and playful. Some members are outgoing and friendly while others remain shy and introspective. A continuum from passive to highly competitive natures can be observed in every facet of cult life. Moonies are not singlemindedly dedicated to their religious beliefs. They retain their personal interests and often develop new hobbies while serving their cause. Animated discussions which range over such diverse topics as skiing, politics, rock music, folk dancing, oil painting, engineering, and karate can be heard in a single evening at Unification Church centers.

Stereotype 2.) Moonies are incapable of thinking for themselves

The widespread belief that Moonies are unthinking robots under the control of Reverend Moon or his delegate is not based on fact. It is true that the cult membership idealizes Moon and looks up to him for guidance in all spiritual matters. Similarly, Moon exerts enormous control over each member's destiny and position within the movement. From a Moonie's perspective however, this is a highly logical series of events. In order to become a Unification Church member, one must believe that

Reverend Moon is (at the very least) God's spokesman on earth. Therefore, to disobey Moon is to disobey God.

Nevertheless, few members totally acquiesce to all the movement's stringent rules and some become openly defiant. One female member described her reaction to a suggestion that she not telephone her parents. "When I got in, they said it wouldn't be good to call your parents because your parents are against the church...Well, I said to myself, 'I'll call my parents regardless of whether you like it or not. You don't be telling me not to call my mother.'"

Members think, discuss, read, and agonize over the appropriateness of their values and belief system. There is not an accepted universal interpretation of every aspect of the Divine Principle. Each member formulates his unique belief system according to his own synthesis and understanding of the Church's philosophic approach. "The Divine Principle," one male Moonie related, "is only the bones of the structure. It's up to each member to fill in the meat."

Undeniably, intense pressure is placed on members to obey the dictates of their superiors. Moonies quickly realize that obedience results in promotions. Most members recognize that their superiors in the movement are not infallible and they silently question the correctness of every directive they receive. If they aspire to rise within the movement, however, they must obey. This has led to some rather painful consequences as one former Moonie recalled. "(They had) these bizarre rituals that made absolutely no sense and deliberately so. I mean, you have gone into this restaurant twice the same evening and the bouncer says 'You come in here again and I'm going to break your face.' You go out and the team captain looks at you and says 'You go back in there again. If you have faith you can do it.'" That members are willing to obey a foolish or destructive order results not from blind trust in their superiors' decision making ability but rather a frantic desire for promotion within the movement. Assigned to the rigors of the lowly mobile fundraising teams, many members are desperate to advance to more comfortable positions. To get ahead one must cooperate and be a team player. Thus, what society perceives as unthinking acceptance of any order, Moonies logically view as the quickest route to promotion.

Stereotype 3.) Moonies are humorless.

The nature of the Moonies' interaction with society is frequently intense. Neither group trusts the motivation of the other so that conversations are, more often that not, fraught with mutual tension. These conditions are not conducive to the development of a comfortable, relaxed atmosphere in which humor normally resides. Consequently, the pubic assumes that Moonies have no sense of humor. Within the confines of their own group, however, genuine laughter is a common occurrence. Many Moonies have an excellent sense of humor and love to amuse their fellow members. Moonies appreciate a keen wit, particularly if it turns its cutting edge toward those who persecute them. Nevertheless, members can and frequently do laugh at themselves as well. Humor expressed by the Moonies ranges from gentle individual teasing to elaborate renderings of classic literary humor, presented in a professional style.

Stereotype 4.) All Moonies have a glassy eyed stare resulting from their brainwashed condition.

Lined up one by one, Moonies would be indistinguishable from a group of their conservative college counterparts. The basis for the glassy eyed stare myth originated in the early years of the movement. Members were encouraged to pursue zealously new recruits and money at a hectic pace. To achieve bloated quotas, members frequently existed on very little sleep. Consequently they were meeting

the public with the bleary eyed countenance of
the exhausted. A longstanding member of the
Church remembered those grueling early years:
"In the short run we had to make a kind of
desperate effort to build our foundation quickly
and establish a nationwide movement in a few
years. That was a sacrifice that the members
made willingly. But we had to pay a price in
terms of pubic relations. And some members did
get hurt by being pushed too hard by their
leaders. So we made some mistakes too and now we
are paying for them--but I think it was worth it
in the long run."

Stereotype 5.) Moonies work constantly for
their religion and never relax.

        Moonies are dedicated to furthering the
goals of their movement. Toward this end, most
members expend considerable time and energy
during their day. To assume however, that
members work continuously to the exclusion of
pleasant recreational activities is incorrect.
Moonies enjoy frequent breaks from the challenge
of their religious work. Lengthy meal times,
after dinner games and frequent group sing
alongs are a daily staple of Moonies residing in
Church organized facilities. Special projects
occasionally arise which require a concentrated
expenditure of group work. Nevertheless, any
extended periods of total work are likely to be
an individual's self imposed standard rather
than the group's demand.

Stereotype 6.) Moonies are forced to break off
relations with their families.

        During the initial months following their
religious conversion, new members may be
encouraged to withhold the knowledge of their
membership from unsympathetic parents. Moonies
believe that the recently converted are in a
stage of spiritual infancy and highly vulnerable
to antagonistic outside forces. Consequently
members are wary of the potential influence
wielded by a convert's family. History has
shown that alarmed American parents have proved
to be worthy opponents of the Unification

Church. Abductions and deprogramming efforts, carried out with the precision and daring of wartime commando raids have effectively cut into the ranks of the Church membership.

Nevertheless, Moonies maintain a firm belief in the sanctity of the family unit. The Divine Principle teaches that the family is the ideal composition for man to become one with God. Therefore, if parents willingly accept their offsprings' commitment to the Church, cult members are encouraged to maintain strong family ties. Dissolution of familial attachment results more frequently from parents' reluctance to defer to their child's commitment to the Church rather than an anti-family cult directive.

The disintegration of close family ties (if it occurs) is perhaps the most difficult aspect of cult existence for the membership. Moonies are deeply saddened by the anguish that their family members experience as a result of their conversion. Further, they are upset that their parents fail to recognize the validity of their work or the idealistic scope of their dream. To the convert, however, commitment to his religious ideals must supersede any personal allegiance, no matter how painful.

CULT RECRUITMENT

CHAPTER IX

EAST COAST/WEST COAST

"In the long run we have to meet the nation as who we are--not some group who picks up travellers from off the street who don't know anything about us."

- a 32 year old Moonie

"They have their roots of schism in the organization right now. There is a west coast tradition and an east coast tradition. And with Moon out of the picture, it could be split up in many ways."

- a 25 year old former Moonie

In discussing the recruitment process of the Unification Church, one must acknowledge some important distinctions between the methods employed by the west coast centers as compared to centers on the east coast.

During the initial years of the Church's development in the United States, California became the primary focus for most of the movement's activities. Blessed with pleasant year-round weather, several large universities, and an atmosphere that attracted disenchanted youth; California was the logical headquarters for the cult's massive recruitment operations. At the center of these operations was (and is) the powerful Oakland chapter, the largest group center in the Unification Church's

constellation. Under the sophisticated
direction of the chapter leader, Moses Durst,
the Oakland center perfected the early
recruitment system. Thousands of recruits were
exposed to the Church's doctrine as a result of
the tenacious efforts of the Oakland membership.
Today, despite the growth of the cult into
almost every major city in the nation, the
Oakland center remains the primary recruitment
arm of the Church. A former member described a
typical reaction to the Oakland center's
recruitment program. "The group in California
is very together in terms of their recruiting.
Slick, sophisticated old timers who have been
there for many years and really know their
stuff. They have a really quality program
there."

The east coast movement, on the other
hand, lacks the depth, experience, and complex
recruitment machinery of the west coast chapter.
Plagued by intemperate weather for much of the
year, east coast chapters cannot make use of the
isolated outdoor settings which have proved so
instrumental to the conversion process. East
coast Moonies are forced to conduct information
and indoctrination seminars in cramped area
centers. Seated on battered folding chairs amid
the stark atmosphere of the center, many
recruits' initial enthusiasm dissolves into a
realistic appraisal of the Church's demanding
life-style. More importantly, perhaps, the east
coast centers lack an area leader who can match
the awesome magnetic appeal of Moses Durst.
Fledgling recruits often maintain enthusiasm for
the movement because the leaders can express the
idealistic principles in an exciting way.
"Everyone is impressed by Moses," a former
Moonie related. "He's so very special, so
sincere, so intelligent. You say to yourself--
Well, if he's involved; it must be O.K."

There are, however, more fundamental
differences between the two groups' recruitment
techniques. The east coast Moonies clearly
identify their affiliation with the Unification
Church. Centers prominently display large
photographs of Reverend Moon. The membership

proudly promote their beliefs in a
straightforward open manner. The west coast
centers are frequently more deceptive as one
high ranking C.A.R.P. official explains.
"There's different styles of recruiting. People
in the Oakland group tended to be very indirect
and invite people over without telling them that
it is associated with Reverend Moon. It wasn't
until after a week of being involved in the
seminars that they learned that is was Reverend
Moon."

In the following discussion of the
Unification Church's recruitment techniques,
emphasis will be placed on the California
(Oakland) method. The reason for this decision
is threefold.

1) California was and is the major
recruitment center for the Church.

2) Every former Unification Church
member who agreed to participate in this
study was converted in the California
recruitment system.

3) From a psychological perspective the
California recruitment style is more
complex and interesting than the east
coast method.

To assume, however, that this is the only
recruitment method employed by the Unification
Church is to deny the complexity of the
movement. While the Oakland group uses
deception (through omission of their
affiliation), the east coast Moonies attempt to
take advantage of the notoriety their reputation
has created. The advertisement on the following
page was widely distributed on the University of
Michigan campus in the fall of 1980.

86

You thought you'd seen everything.

But, now :

PRIME FORCE

strikes ⊕ again!!

ROCK- THE NEWEST WAVE

Blow your own concepts.
Guess who's putting it on...
Moonies! (GASP)

It's not what you'd expect but,
it's definitely worth checking out.

After all, it's not everyday that you
see a Moonie band.   UM-CARP

Tues. Dec. 9 – Noon
M. Union Assembly Hall

No charge; but the room ain't large,
so come early.

CHAPTER X

BRIEF OVERVIEW OF THE RECRUITMENT PROCESS

"I was determined that day to change my
life--to change everything. I wanted to throw
out my old life and start all over again."

                        - a 24 year old female
                        Moonie on the eve of her
                        first church contact

        The procedure for the recruiting and
proselytizing efforts of the Unification Church
generally follows a well established, successful
pattern of interaction between the cult
recruiter and his unwary target. A typical
recruitment effort may be characterized as
follows.

        An extremely friendly, sincere recruiter
will approach a young person and attempt to
engage him in a conversation. The setting,
whether it be a restaurant, street, bus station,
or movie theater is irrelevant to the
recruiter's basic tactic of developing a one-to-
one conversation with the young person. Visual
cues such as a guitar, backpack, or books often
provide the initial stimulus for an opening
remark that may lead to a discussion. This
technique is referred to by the cult as
"establishing a common base." The recruiter
attempts to create the impression of intense
interest and curiosity about any activity or
person that is important to the youth. "If a

person said that he had just got through reading the owner's manual for a '64 Chevy (observed one former Moonie tongue-in-cheek), they would say 'That's fascinating, that's my favorite book.'," Initially the recruiter makes no attempt to express or push his convictions onto the youth. On the contrary, he tries to learn what the young person thinks about a variety of subjects, rarely related to religion, cults, or the Unification Church.

If the youth appears at all receptive to the conversation with the recruiter he is invited to a dinner at the Church's neighborhood house. The dinners are always pleasant affairs carefully staged and designed to display the feelings of friendliness and love between the members. The potential recruit is showered with attention and affection and made to feel like an extremely important and interesting person.

Dinner is followed by a lively session of music, singing and a high spirited lecture. The content of the lecture, while slightly tinged with religious idealism, generally expresses the notion that the world could be a better place. Presented in an upbeat, enthusiastic style, the lecture contains mostly simplistic cliches and platitudes which few people can find fault with.

Throughout the evening the recruit is subtly reinforced for conforming thoughts and behavior while inappropriate responses (such as questioning the group's motives, etc.) elicit attitudes of sadness and disappointment from members. At no time during the evening is the Unification Church, religion, or Reverend Moon mentioned to the potential recruit.

At the conclusion of the evening the recruit is invited to attend a weekend workshop to get to know his new friends better and learn about their interesting movement.

The workshop is extremely cheap ($15, free to those who can't afford it) and all arrangements from transportation to housing are prearranged by the group. Recalcitrant recruits are often enticed by the promise of a weekend escape filled with quiet rural beauty away from the fast paced pressures of their urban life.

The weekend workshops however prove to be less than idyllic with almost every minute of the recruit's time taken up by lectures, singing, physical activities, and small group discussions. All workshop activities are carefully structured and orchestrated to reorient the recruit to a new way of looking at the world. As with all stages in the recruitment process, knowledge about the cult is parceled out in a slow, meticulous manner, giving the recruit only as much information as he needs to know to accomplish each step in the indoctrination procedure.

Members employ a variety of techniques, including the use of an extensive reward system of affection and attention, to achieve their purpose of eventually converting the recruit. The isolation of the camp along with the complete loss of individual privacy contribute to the recruit's growing feeling of disorientation and loss of control. Exhaustive schedules maintained by both recruits and members offer little opportunity for any kind of meaningful reflection or thoughtful introspection about the events or psychological changes occurring during the workshop.

Tremendous energy is devoted to group activities such as singing, recreational games, and discussions to stimulate a sense of cohesion and togetherness among workshop participants. The lectures are designed to be inspirational and hint at a body of knowledge that not only offers individual peace and happiness, but also provides answers to world problems

By Sunday night, many recruits are eager to learn more and members encourage everyone to stay at the camp for an additional week long workshop.

If the recruit attends the week long workshop the same basic conditions that

prevailed during the weekend encounter are
maintained, but at an even more intense level.
It is during this week long workshop that many
recruits learn for the first time that the group
they are interacting with is a part of the
Unification Church.

The procedure of indoctrination to the
cult's principles is presented in an aggressive
yet earnest manner by polished lecturers. The
recruit is bombarded with a daily series of
lectures, and group discussions designed to
educate him quickly and effectively to the
tenets of the group's philosophy.

Techniques designed to arouse feelings of
guilt, shame, and childlike dependency are
utilized in the isolated setting of the group's
camp. Critical analysis of the Unification
Church's goals, practices, or philosophy is
strongly discouraged as are skepticism and
negative evaluations of members.

Eventually, the recruit is brought to a
state of high emotional tension by the group
through a series of cleverly orchestrated
activities. It is at this point that receptive
recruits are pressed by members for a full time
commitment to the cult. Less responsive
recruits are strongly encouraged to participate
in an additional week of lectures and
discussions, very similar to the first week's
program so the Moonies may try again to bring
about the hoped for conversion.

At the culmination of the second week's
workshop, recruits are again urged to become
full time members of the Unification Church.
For most recruits the second week-long
experience has either convinced them to become
members or to leave the group altogether.
Occasionally, a recalcitrant recruit will attend
a third week of lectures and activities if group
members perceive that his reluctance is based on
indecision rather than skepticism or
indifference to the group.

Frequently, those who decide not to join the cult are aggressively urged by members to return for another workshop session at some later date. Members rarely completely give up the hope of converting any recruit who shows a strong interest in membership. One recruit who decided not to join the cult gives the following account of his later experience with Moonie recruiters:

"The first couple of weeks, I would keep running into those people I'd seen up there--(at the training camp) on the streets of San Francisco. They would ask me when I was coming back and I would say I'm not sure. One of them said, 'You know, no one will ever love you as much as we do.' One of the things that they did was tap into people's insecurities and feelings of not being loved--and traded on that."

CHAPTER XI

THE RECRUITER

"We are asking young people to sacrifice their youth for God."

                    - a 20 year old Moonie

"You gradually learn how to do it the right way and the wrong way. How to go up to a total stranger and act like you'd known them all your life--be familiar with them. I have this view in my head that you don't respect people's boundaries. You feel like--we're all brothers and sisters--all related in one big, happy family. It's just that they don't know it yet."

                    - a 26 year old former Moonie

During the recruitment process, all Unification Church members strive to present an image of themselves as mature, socially committed young people. The cult is well aware that initial attitudes are influenced not only by behavior but also by the nature of the characteristics that people possess. Thus, members maintain an attractive, well scrubbed persona that is calculated to maximize the most favorable response from others in terms of trust and receptivity.

Male cult members' hair is cut neatly short and few members retain the beards or moustaches they grew before joining the cult.

Female members are attractively dressed with a minimum of makeup or jewelry. Clothes are clean, pressed and lack any hint of flamboyance. The Unification Church, like other businesses which deal with the public, has learned that the presentation of a clean cut, conservative image tends to inspire confidence in others.

Similarly, Moonies often convey the impression of inner tranquility through an outward appearance of calm. They rarely lose their composure in public even under trying circumstances. This appearance of outward calm, however, does not suggest that the membership lacks enthusiasm. On the contrary, many recruits appear to be initially drawn to cult members as a result of their energetic countenance. A former cult member explained his attraction to a cult recruiter.

"She was so...laid back - kind of calm - yet stimulating. I felt I needed to be near her...not on a sexual level you understand - but she was electric...(she) lit me up with her approach."

CHAPTER XII

THE INITIAL ENCOUNTER

"Tell me and I'll listen. I will hear what you have to say. If it makes more sense than what I'm doing...I may absorb some of it."

            - a 26 year old former Moonie

"The only way you could get off the streets and into an administrative job was to be successful. They (Moonies) were desperate to get a member. Just frantic...you just weren't successful unless you brought somebody to dinner every night."

            - a 25 year old former Moonie

For the experienced Moonie recruiter, the first encounter with a potential recruit (be it a carefully contrived introduction or a spontaneous street meeting) involves the application of a personally ritualized system of successful psychological techniques. At this initial confrontation the recruiter must capture and hold the attention of a stranger, impress him with his sincerity and secure a commitment from him for a future involvement. To accomplish these aims the recruiter relies on three primary methods:

1) building affective bonds with the recruit,

2) locating and tapping into the idealistic and redemptive needs of the recruit, and

3) employing deception techniques.

Building Affective Bonds

In order to make a favorable impression on a uninterested stranger, the recruit realizes that he must make his initial meeting exciting or interesting for his target. The most obvious, yet disarmingly effective, practice employed by Moonies is to provide prospective recruits with rewards far in excess of their expectations for the situation. Individuals, Walster (1971) observed, are attracted to and like others who reward them. Attention and praise are heaped indiscriminately upon the startled but nevertheless flattered target. For his part, the recruiter struggles to maintain the impression of rapt interest in the potential recruit's every thought. He manipulates the conversation to insure that the target gets lavishly rewarded for discussing his favorite topic--himself. In the presence of this insightful person who recognizes his heretofore ignored qualities, the recruit begins to feel important--perhaps even fascinating.

Frequently, the recruiter is a member of the opposite sex which heightens the experience by adding an unspoken but recognized element of sexuality to the interaction. While Moonies eschew overt sexual come-ons in their recruitment practices they occasionally employ a mild form of flirting to establish an initial contact. One former member recalled,

"It worked better from female to male than the other way around. Some of them would walk up and put their arm through some guy's arm or grab his hand or

something like that. Kind of cute--
nothing lurid about--kind of like junior
high teasing."

Once the initial contact is cemented Church
members make no effort to capitalize on any
sexual overtones implicit in their interaction.
To a lonely young recruit, however, this
exhilarating interest by a member of the
opposite sex may be mistakenly viewed as
personal or sexual attraction.

At some convenient point in the
interaction process, the recruiter will attempt
to probe subtly the target's emotional defense
structure to learn what he most values, fears,
and hopes for in life. By securing some insight
into the target's emotional perspective, the
recruiter expands his control within the current
interaction context. More importantly however,
he collects useful information that may be
exploited to the cult's advantage during
subsequent interactions. Areas of particular
interest to the target are systematically
pursued by the recruiter who feigns conspicuous
enthusiasm for the topic. Conversely, areas of
dissimilarity or disagreement with the target's
values, interests, or lifestyle are studiously
avoided. The recruiter labors to promote the
impression of commonality between himself and
the potential recruit. This technique Byrne
(1968, 1971) discovered is an exceedingly
effective system for establishing affective
bonds between strangers. In an intensive
research program with various associates, Byrne
found evidence of a positive linear relationship
between attraction to a stranger and the
proportion of attitudes held in common with that
stranger. Similarity of attitudes, Byrne
theorizes, provides the individual with
independent evidence of the correctness of his
interpretation of social reality--a kind of
validation of his point of view.

Ordinarily, the target should be
naturally suspicious of a one sided relationship
in which he receives an abundance of rewards
while investing very little effort. Flattery,

however, when deftly executed, is rarely detected by those to whom it is directed. The flattered youth finds nothing odd about a relationship which appears to offer no discernible benefits to the other party. He simply assumes that the recruiter has recognized him for the fascinating person he always knew himself to be.

The recruiter provides his target with as little information about himself and the organization he represents as possible. West coast recruiters rarely volunteer information about their association with the Unification Church or provide any other information which might frighten off their prospect.

The recruiter's end goal during this initial encounter is to commit the unsuspecting target to some future, more structured interactions with the Church membership. This commitment is generally elicited by extending a "spontaneous" invitation to dinner where the recruit can meet and talk with like minded friends. Recruiters endeavor to sketch a stimulating yet vague portrait of the group-- preferring to allow the potential recruit's imagination to fill in the details. A former Moonie with five years of recruitment experience related her customary closing remarks to a target:

> "If you could only see what we do. Come over to our house for dinner...It's a community but it's really hard to explain. Come over and just meet some of the people--experience the atmosphere-- then you will understand what I'm talking about."

Those targets not eager to retain this new found association often feel obligated to some future interaction as a result of the pleasant personal interest shown by the recruiter. Although reluctant, they may accept a dinner invitation to avoid appearing rude.

100

Tapping into Idealistic and Redemptive Needs

A second method of securing a favorable reaction from potential recruits is to tap into their mystical, idealistic or redemptive interests.

Young people, particularly college students, are emotionally besieged by philosophic and religious questions which unfold in association with their identity formation. During this period, most youth struggle to formulate a coherent set of ideals and standards which will provide stability and meaning to their lives. Idealistic young people are seldom satisfied with the existing world order or their position in it. "Youth," Erikson (1968) observed, "is sensitive to any suggestion that it may be hopelessly determined by what went before it in life histories or in history." (p.247)

The young frequently mistrust adult generations. Neither their leaders nor their institutions provide the inflexibly idealistic young person with identification models or an ideology capable of inspiring impassioned commitment. Rebellion against the entrenched adult institutions left one male former member amenable to more youthful solutions to the world's problems at the time of his conversion.

"I was rebelling against established religion--established anything. Because I believed that we (youth) could do it better, that there was a better way of doing it." Earlier in the same conversation he observed, "I was very open to people who had a new way-- extremely inquisitive and curious-- dissatisfied. I could not be part of the system."

Young people often prefer to look toward their own age mates to resolve and reformulate philosophic and religious strategies for life in the modern world. As a result the Unification Church provides regular forums for interested young people to meet with youthful members to discuss issues that intrigue or trouble them. A tactic used with stunning success by the recruiters involves posing a thought provoking question as an introduction. "Which do you think will save the world: Science, Religion, or Politics?" Having broken the ice with this intriguing overture, the recruiter will pursue a philosophical discussion with the youth. Introductory questions are seldom explicitly religious in tone or content to avoid frightening off wary young targets. Nevertheless, the questions are framed so that one might logically respond in a religious or idealistic manner if so inclined.

In addition to providing an easy ice breaker, the philosophic inquiry accommodates other cult recruitment strategies. The question serves as a convenient weeding out device for those youth whose philosophic or religious attitudes are so contrary to those of the cult that they are unlikely prospects for an eventual conversion experience. For those individuals whose response more closely coincides with the Church's philosophy the question often opens a floodgate of personal information. By listening closely to the target's response, the recruiter can often garner valuable insights into the potential recruit's problems, interests, and aspirations.

As with all first encounters the recruiter's end goal is casually to invite the target back to the Church center for dinner. Closing remarks such as "That's an interesting point, let's discuss it over dinner at my house" frequently accomplish this aim.

Deception Techniques

Moonies are painfully aware of the notoriety associated with their religious movement. As the "one, true religion", Moonies firmly believe that the cause of their unflattering public images emerges out of the devil's satanic efforts to destroy their church and its credibility forever. Their perception of the awesome power wielded by their adversary (Satan) has led some zealous Church members to advocate using any means at their command in order to defeat him. This philosophy (widely practiced on the west coast) has produced several reported cases of deceptive recruiting. Referred to as "heavenly deception", members legitimize the use of less than honest practices by pointing out the deplorable alternative--a satanically controlled world. While personally reprehensible to them, Moonies believe that in this special case, the end justifies the means. One former member explained the Moonie rationale for deceiving recruits as follows:

> "It was like an Orwellian thing--where yes is no and no is yes--the truth is a lie and a lie is the truth. If I were to tell people yes, we have a religious belief--we follow Reverend Sun Myung Moon--that's the truth--but it's a lie because people are going to respond to that with negativity. They are going to respond to that based on negative information that they had from Time magazine or they are going to respond based on their own sinful nature--and they won't join. So if I tell them the truth, then it's really a lie because they would be responding to lies. So if I lie to them and say, 'Oh, it's a wonderful organization, we are into service projects'--that are nonexistent objectively--that's a lie, but it's really the truth because we are saving people spiritually and we are building an entire new world. And in the end this

will be the ultimate effect. So I can
lie to you and say, 'No, we are not
Moonies, please give' and in the end feel
confident that if we are not doing it
now, sometime we would be. We had the
ultimate answer, the final truth."

The most commonly practiced recruitment
deception involves the use of numerous front
organizations that attract potential recruits
with ideological and mystical sounding titles.
To overcome their notorious image in the United
States Moonies felt compelled to disguise their
organizational roots from outsiders. Only after
a recruit was firmly entrenched in the
Unification philosophy and value system was he
told that the groups was in fact the Unification
Church. [At no time during the author's
interaction with the Unification Church did any
member attempt to misrepresent the movement's
identity.] Commonly used west coast Moonie
front organizations include: Creative Community
Project (formerly known as New Education
Development Systems Inc. and the International
Re-Education Foundation), The Center for Ethical
Management and Planning, and the One World
Crusade.

CHAPTER XIII

THE DINNER MEETING

"We rolled over to the center and I walked inside. There are all these lights on and it was like you walked out of the darkness into the daylight. And all these people were saying, 'hi, good to see you, hi'. In my mind I said, 'What the heck is all this? All these people smiling'."

- a 28 year old Moonie

"It never struck me that it was religious--not a hint. That's why I went. I thought it was a community communal project. You know, people living together, working together, eating together."

- a 25 year old former Moonie

The dinner meeting plays a pivotal role in the Unification Church recruitment process. Carefully staged and orchestrated, the meeting is designed to accomplish four essential purposes:

1) serve as a pre-selection vehicle for more intense future recruitment interaction;

2) provide an environment conducive to a favorable first impression of the group;

3) generate increased interest and curiosity in the cult's lifestyle and goals; and

4) elicit commitments from individual recruits for the weekend seminars.

Pre-selection vehicle

Moonies are well aware that their movement has limited appeal to most members of society. They have come to realize that initial involvement with the cult (often under questionable pretenses) provides no guarantee that a potential recruit might not be extremely disruptive in future interactions. Therefore, the dinner meeting provides a comfortable, low key atmosphere in which members can observe and evaluate the likelihood that a particular recruit will comply with more regimented church indoctrination techniques.

The willingness with which an individual acquiesces to minor social demands of the group provides the membership with important clues regarding his probable future reactions to more intense recruitment activities. A "spiritually prepared" recruit is one who readily complies with all group requests and appears eager to learn more about the movement. If an individual, on the other hand, balks at complying with relatively minor group requests such as removing his shoes at the door or making a donation for dinner (even though the original invitation made no mention of cost) he is generally eliminated from future cult activities. His reluctant attitude may prove counterproductive to the cult's overall recruitment process.

For those recruits who are "spiritually prepared" the dinner meeting provides the initial opportunity for them to learn their role within the group and begin to assimilate appropriate attitudes. Members place potential recruits in situations that frequently require them either to comply passively with the group's wishes or be rude through an open display of defiance. A self conscious recruit, for example, who is embarrassed by the group sing along will be continuously encouraged by members to participate until he either acquiesces against his will or vociferously refuses. The recruit begins to realize two important group principles which accompany total acceptance. He must be willing to subvert his personal preference to that of the collective. Secondly, he must be willing to conform completely to the group's expectations of his behavior. The dinner meeting, therefore, provides the recruit with a mild introduction to the cult's future expectations of his behavior and his role within the group. For both the Moonies and the recruit, the dinner meeting serves as a weeding out process which greatly eases the transition to the more rigorous weekend seminar.

Promoting a Favorable Impression

For most recruits the dinner meeting provides their initial contact with the collective membership and the home environment of the movement. The impression that the recruits carry away may be the single most important factor determining the extent of their future involvement with the cult. Consequently, the dinner meeting has evolved into a carefully planned affair designed to maximize the group's appealing characteristics.

Once the potential converts enter the Unification Church center they are surrounded by the warmth and friendship of the "Family". Techniques such as love bombings, where recruits are inundated with a constant flow of attention, praise and flattery create the illusion that the cult truly likes them. "I was more welcome there," observed one former Moonie, "than I was with my own family. There they were all interested in me." The aggressive use of love bombing techniques to create a positive impression is based on firm psychological

107

foundations. The results of studies in social psychological research (Byrne 1968, 1971) indicate that people tend to like others in a direct linear relationship to the proportion of positive reinforcements they receive or can expect to receive from those others. Thus, an overwhelming bombardment of positive reinforcement by the cult membership promotes a favorable environment for the unsuspecting recruit's immediate acceptance of the group.

The dinner itself is a very pleasant affair involving plenty of nourishing food, discussion and open camaraderie. The meal is often served on a long, low table with participants seated on the floor--which tends to enhance the impression of the non-traditional nature of the group. Frequent displays of affection, concern, and interest between members further embellish the image of the family type structure of the movement. One pretty cult member described her initial reaction to the group's appearance of togetherness this way: "What I thought was really neat was that they were all happy, they were all smiling, they all had good things to say about one another."

The underlying message the membership attempts to convey to each potential recruit is that "we are an interesting and exciting family group who can and will fulfill all your social and emotional needs if you simply allow us to."

Generating Increased Interest in the Group

While the primary thrust of the evening is social, members are eager to portray the ideological intent of their movement. A major function of the dinner meeting is to allow the membership to impress upon the recruits the notion that they are held together by an important sense of purpose and mission. This process is accomplished by a rousing after dinner lecture, noted more for its spirited, upbeat delivery than for any controversial ideas within its content. These well rehearsed

lectures allude to the establishment of a solid
ideological framework in vague, generalized
terms designed to arouse the recruits'
curiosity. This technique of maintaining
potential recruits in a perpetual state of
uncertainty regarding the group's ideological
direction serves two useful purposes for the
cult. First, it allows the membership to parcel
out their unorthodox philosophy in small
manageable doses that are less likely to
frighten off the uninitiated. Second, by
shrouding their group in a cloak of mystery and
investing its membership with a sense of
mystical importance, the cult enhances its own
image while generating considerable curiosity
among the recruits. Neither the content nor the
delivery of these after dinner speeches changes
much from one meeting to the next as one former
member recalls: "There would be this ritual;
these lectures given in the same way with the
same jokes in the same places and large groups
of members who have heard it so many times
before, just struggling to stay awake--pinching
themselves and everything to perk up and laugh
uproariously at these lines."
    The lecture itself and the members'
enthusiastic support of its contents serves
three important purposes. First, it provides
the recruits with their initial impression of
the group's deeper purpose. By presenting a
philosophy (albeit a very watered down version)
the cult acknowledges its primary reason for
existence. The lecture's innocent content may
lead some recruits to assume that the group's
philosophy is rooted in conventional thought.
Thereafter they may become less wary of the
philosophic intent. Second, the membership's
enthusiastic support of the lecture graphically
illustrates to the recruits the intensity of the
group's commitment to "a philosophy". Third, a
common philosophy implies a common interest and
a sense of community. Hitler (1939) recognized
the importance of this collective desire among
prospective recruits. "The mass meeting is
necessary, if only for the reason that in it the
individual who is becoming an adherent of a new
movement feels lonely and is easily seized with
the fear of being alone, receives for the first

109

time the pictures of a greater community, something that has a strengthening and encouraging effect on most people." (p.715)

Thus, the recruits leave the dinner meeting with a recognition of the group's deeper commitment to a philosophy. They are completely unaware however, of its intent, purpose, or conceptual structure.

Elicit a Future Commitment

The end goal of the dinner meeting is to elicit a verbal commitment from each acceptable recruit to attend the upcoming weekend seminars. It is at these seminars that the conversion process is conducted in earnest. The cult members utilize two basic approaches to elicit compliance from reluctant recruits. First, the members place recruits in situations where it is difficult to refuse the group's request. To decline the weekend seminar invitation after being invited, doted upon and informed of the group's altruistic commitment to a better world is often difficult for people. Americans are socialized throughout their lives to avoid hurting the feelings of others. The membership makes no attempt to relieve the recruit's sense of guilt or embarrassment over his lack of interest in a group that has been kind to him. The cleverly designed format of the dinner meeting provides no convenient or polite time for a non-interested guest to make a face-saving excuse and leave unobtrusively. On the contrary, a recruit's refusal to make a firm commitment to the weekend seminar generally results in a highly visible and embarrassing scene. A former member discussed his reluctance to be impolite to the cult members during the dinner meeting. Shortly thereafter he joined the group and stayed for three years.

"I came from...this kind of middle class, nice guy, sort of family, the small town thing that you're never rude with anyone, especially someone who is nice. I didn't

110

want to hurt their feelings. I thought I
was doing them a favor by not being rude
to them or try to talk them out of what
they believe. It seems to be good for
them, I'll just play along until the time
comes for me to make my excuse and
leave."

Individuals and group members utilize a
variety of approaches to coax, and override a
reluctant recruit's objections. Disapproval
over the recruit's decision is expressed in
looks of hurt and betrayal designed to make the
offender feel guilt and responsibility. Members
frequently offer to resolve scheduling conflicts
by suggesting practical alternatives or asking
the recruit to evaluate the relative importance
of the previously scheduled activity when
compared with the potential benefits of
continuing his relationship with the group.
Many surprised recruits eventually capitulate to
the cult's demands because they are simply not
prepared to deal with the intensity of the
membership's collective resolve.

A second method used by the Moonies to
elicit a commitment from reluctant recruits to
attend a weekend seminar involves a subtle
psychological technique of escalation. Aronson
(1980) noted that when an individual commits
himself in a small way to a project it increases
the likelihood that he will commit himself
further in that direction. Thus, the dinner
meeting format is designed to require recruits
to make small but ever increasing commitments to
the group as the evening progresses. From the
initial request to pay for dinner (voluntarily)
to the final request to agree with the content
of the non-controversial lecture, the recruit is
subtly being manipulated to commit himself to
the group's values. Consequently, by the end of
the evening many recruits have begun not only to
establish a pattern of acquiescence to group
pressure but also to feel a sense of involvement
and commitment to the cult. Once "softened up"
the recruit finds it much easier to agree to the
more serious commitment of the weekend seminar.

111

CHAPTER XIV

WEEKEND WORKSHOP

"I would ask questions and they would say 'Wait until the lectures.' They are stalling. Everyday that you stay in their program is a day that it's harder to get out. You get attached to the people...attached to the spirit of the group."

                    - a 25 year old former Moonie

"The entertainment was great. You know I got up there and played my guitar. They treat you like you're doing a Bach number on the piano, which was great. There was a lot of ego boosting involved. At first you don't realize it consciously, you just feel good. It's funny, I didn't see it as flattery. Of course afterwards I did. I guess in that sense I was naive."

                    - a 26 year old former Moonie

The weekend workshop is an intense, carefully structured indoctrination seminar designed by the membership to convert pliant recruits to a total commitment of the Unification Church's value system and lifestyle. Frequently conducted in beautiful rural surroundings, the workshop organizers strive to create an exotic ambiance, far removed from the recruits' customary existence. Throughout the weekend participants sleep in spartan, but rustically pleasant, makeshift buildings. Males

and females are strictly segregated from one
another except during cult sanctioned
activities. Each morning recruits and members
wake to the sounds of guitars playing and
'spontaneous' group sing alongs. The cult often
attaches its own Moonie oriented lyrics to
familiar melodies--subtly imposing its
perspective on unsuspecting recruits. After a
brisk session of morning calisthenics and a
nutritious breakfast the daily recruitment
schedule begins in earnest. The recruits'
entire day at the camp is systematically
structured by the cult membership. Their time
is broken down into an ordered series of
activities which include lectures, small group
discussions, exercise, meals, competitive games,
and group social interaction sessions. The
weekend has been organized so that activities
dominate the recruits' schedule from morning
through evening. The intensity of the
workshop's timetable allows participants few
opportunities to attend to personal interests
and precludes occasions for thoughtful
reflection on the day's activities. Recruits
are expected to adhere faithfully to the group's
imposed regimentation of their schedule and
conform to the rules of the workshop. This
includes mandatory attendance at all scheduled
activities. Outside communication such as
magazines, radios, or telephones is greatly
restricted for recruits while attending the
session. Should the recruit have any questions
or concerns while at the camp, he is instructed
to direct them toward his "spiritual parent".
Each recruit is assigned a Moonie mentor before
attending the workshop who looks after the
fledgling recruit and acts as his spiritual
advisor, guide and confidant.

A former Unification Church recruit
provides a more detailed account of the workshop
setting as he recalls his first night at the
Booneville camp in California: "On Friday night
we met over in San Francisco. There were
several large buses. As soon as you got in
there, there was a definite structure to what
was going on. Everything was always focused in
some way or another. So we got on the bus and

we immediately began to sing songs. It was
supposed to be a 2 1/2 or 3 hour bus ride.
Well, we left at 7:30 and pulled in around 12:30
to this place up around Booneville. The buses
were real slow going over the hills. They were
pretty full. There were at least two buses that
went up, so they were taking maybe 65 people.
Of those, 25 or 30 were new people and 25 or 30
were people already in the organization. They
act as the chaperons. When we got there we all
got out and piled into this very low roofed
building. I found out later that it had been a
chicken coop at one time--a large chicken coop.
It was converted into some kind of barrack
situation and the men slept there. Then there
was a trailer and another building on the
property and the women slept there. So the men
slept out on this basically concrete floor--they
asked you to bring sleeping bags. They had some
bedding there for people who didn't have any.
So we got out our stuff, stretched out and in
about 15 minutes lights were out and we were
going to sleep."

The Camp Environment

        To the casual observer, the rustic
setting, communal games, and frequent sing
alongs might convey the impression of a
pleasantly active weekend retreat. To those
familiar with the social psychological
principles of conformity and group control,
however, the workshop takes on a less amiable
cast and purpose. For them, the workshop
represents a classically efficient
indoctrination vehicle. The intent of the
workshop becomes all too clear--to effect a
conversion experience from naive recruits.

        The use and manipulation of the camp
environment plays a key role in this conversion
process. Moonies recognize that in order to be
converted, recruits must change their
perspective--reorient their reality to that
accepted by the cult membership. To facilitate
this process cult members undertake covert

methods to restructure (cognitively and
emotionally) recruits' original normative
orientation. Isolation, ambiguity, rigid
behavioral control, and regulation of group
excitation levels are used to disarming
effectiveness by experienced Moonie recruiters.

Camp Isolation

        The Moonies' consistent selection of
remote, isolated settings for their weekend
seminars suggests a sophisticated understanding
of the religious conversion process. Isolation,
Moonies realize, when combined with an
unfamiliar environment often creates feelings of
disorientation and confusion among the recruits.
Deprived of their accustomed milieu and normal
support groups (parents, friends, etc.) the
recruits find themselves thrust into a subtle,
but nevertheless total, sense of dependency upon
their hosts. Recruits quickly come to
understand that their basic needs, such as food,
shelter, and companionship, are controlled by
the cult membership. Without any outside source
of communication recruits relinquish vital
control over their environment. They may
believe that their comfort--indeed, their
survival--is dependent upon their hosts'
generosity.

        On a more subtle level, the structured
routine of the seminar schedule eliminates the
need for personal decision making and leads to
feelings of helplessness and inadequacy among
recruits. The ordered existence of the camp
life often reduces recruits to a submissive
childlike pattern of interaction with the more
experienced cult members.

        Recruits can no longer rely on the
established status patterns they developed in
normative society to bring them recognition and
respect. Often the behavior or accomplishments
(education, employment, athletic skills, etc.)
that brought the recruit status in society is
devalued or manifestly at variance with the

Unification Church's established status ideal.
What was highly prized in normative society may
bring sanctions or simply lack of interest in
this novel environment. Consequently, the
compliant recruit discovers that, in order to
lower his anxiety and receive rewards from his
benefactors, he must reorient (at least
temporarily) his status structure to become more
consistent with the cult's prevailing status
order.

Inducing Ambiguity

        In order to affect a successful
conversion, recruits must first be softened up--
made malleable to the cult's formidable shaping
process. Confidence in one's self or one's
belief is a powerful enemy of the religious
conversion method. Consequently, Moonies
endeavor to undermine the recruit's prior
convictions and self assurance at every
opportunity during the weekend seminars.
Inducing a state of ambiguity is perhaps the
most efficacious strategy employed by the cult
membership to accomplish this objective. For
most people ambiguity creates acute feelings of
inadequacy which result in greatly increased
susceptibility to outside influences. Moonie
recruits are no exception. Unsure of their role
and lacking a well defined repertoire of coping
behaviors to deal effectively with their tenuous
position in the group, recruits are often
unnerved. They grasp eagerly at any directive
or advice from an experienced Church member
which will provide them with a stable guideline
for their behavior.

        Moonies strive to create an atmosphere
rife with ambiguity throughout the weekend.
Recruits are never given any information beyond
the amount they will need to accomplish the task
at hand. By minimizing the information it
divulges while simultaneously controlling all
the rewards, the cult is assured of recruits
eager to extirpate their uncertainty. The most
direct method of extinguishing the anxiety

related to ambiguity involves a process known as modeling. The concept of modeling is based upon the psychological principle that when reality is unclear, other people in the environment become a major source of information. In totally ambiguous surroundings (like those at the seminar) the perplexed recruits will logically use the behavior of other people as a template for their own actions. Lacking their own repertoire of appropriate responses to this novel situation, they will likely imitate the competent behavior of the more knowledgeable individuals around them--Moonies. As a result recruits unknowingly establish an emotional and cognitive identification with the cult membership.

Group reinforcement techniques are immediately applied to recruits exhibiting appropriately imitated cult behavior. By collectively rewarding modeled behavior in recruits, members share the burden for the shaping process. More importantly, however, they contribute to the illusion that everyone values this set of behavioral standards. "The power of reward and punishment," Asch (1952) observed, "can determine us to judge the same action as good or bad, true or false. For an organism governed by rewards and punishment these are the only possible and necessary proofs. The laws of learning grind out truth and falsehood indifferently; rewards and punishment are the sole content and criteria of right and wrong." (p.372)

In the isolated setting of camp, with little opportunity to verify their original orientation, some recruits fall prey to the cult shaping program. One former Moonie acknowledged, "It was very difficult to stand back and criticize it. It was a completely unified philosophical perspective that you were sort of enmeshed in--with everyone around you believing this stuff. It was very difficult for you to stand back and get outside of it--almost impossible."

To insure the dominance of their

perspective throughout the workshop, Moonies
segregate recruits from one another except
during regulated group activities. Concerns,
recruits are told, should be expressed to one's
spiritual parent or other knowledgeable members
and not uninformed trainees. Any efforts by
recruits to converse with one another are
swiftly disrupted by cult members, as one former
Moonie recalled. "All the time that this is
going on, you are never with anybody who is not
a member. If two people got together and were
having conversations they would break it up.
They did not want you talking to somebody who
was not convinced that this was the way to go."

In addition to denying recruits an
opportunity to reaffirm their original
perspective, segregation serves other important
cult interests. By separating recruits,
occasions for internal dissension are diminished
while the opportunities for conformity
situations spiral. Asch (1965) noted that a
crucial factor determining the likelihood that
an individual's opinion will conform to that of
the majority is based simply on whether or not
that majority opinion is unanimous. Asch
discovered that if a subject is presented with
even one ally his tendency to conform to an
erroneous judgement by the majority is sharply
reduced. Dissension, Moonies recognize, is
contagious among the ranks of uncertain
recruits. Like any infectious disease it must
be isolated and rooted out privately. The cult
membership strives to create an atmosphere free
of opposing viewpoints in order to surround and
envelop the impressionable recruits in the
unanimity of their perspective. When everyone
around you maintains an identical frame of
reference it may prove exceedingly difficult to
assess critically one's orientation. A former
recruit (male) who came to this realization puts
it this way: "You couldn't think about it or
talk about it with anyone who had any critical
ideas about it. Because everyone that you would
be talking to already believed all this stuff."

119

A parallel can be drawn between the recruits' insulation from condemnatory evaluations of the Unification Church and the equally isolated perspective of the high command that surrounded Hitler during World War II. Albert Speer, a top advisor to Hitler, recounts in his memoirs the sinister implications of unquestioning acceptance of a unique perspective of reality.

> "In normal circumstances, people who turn their backs on reality are soon set straight by the mockery and criticism of those around them. In the Third Reich there was no such correctives. On the contrary, every self deception was multiplied as in a hall of distorting mirrors, becoming a repeatedly confirmed picture of a fantastical dream world which no longer has any relationship to the grim outside world. In those mirrors I could see nothing but my own face reproduced many times over." (p.291)

Rigid Behavioral Control

Moonies wield considerable social pressure in their weekend campaign to influence recruits to adapt their reconstructed world orientation. During the seminars the membership maintains almost total domination over every facet of the recruit's life. Rigid schedules are developed which leave scant opportunity for flexibility or individual initiative. Everyone sleeps, eats, goes to lectures and exercises according to an unbending, cult authored schedule. As a result, compliant recruits are placed in a subordinate childlike position of following orders without input into the decision making process. In essence, the recruit is absolved from any responsibility associated with the success or failure of the weekend events. He need only follow directions and avoid controversy to be reinforced by the cult membership.

The Unification philosophy subtly pervades every aspect of the weekend seminar. Relationships, which generally offer the opportunity for individual idiosyncratic expression, are organized and stereotyped. Efforts to show favoritism in any form are vigorously discouraged. Similarly, intimacy and sexuality are rigidly controlled and ritualized. Displays of sexual interest provoke swift reactions of displeasure and incredulity from the celibate membership. Salacious recruits quickly learn to curb their offensive vocabulary and confine their behavioral perspectives to more androgynous concerns.

On the other hand, efforts directed toward effusiveness and generosity meet with a favorable reaction from Moonies--as long as the gesture is applied equally to all the participants. Mealtime offers an excellent opportunity for a member or recruit to express his munificent nature, as one former Moonie suggested.

"There was a great emphasis on people being warm and loving and always sharing. When they would pass food around, for example, the idea was to take some and give it to somebody else before you ate. I can remember passing plates of sandwiches, breaking one and giving half away--or both away. The idea was to try and give somebody something before they could ask for it."

Recruits are reinforced to recognize that individual demands must be subordinated to the needs of the group. This egalitarian approach to relationships has a two fold advantage for the cult. First, it discourages individual initiative in interpersonal interactions--thus contributing to stereotyped relationships. Second, it often produces a subtle but nevertheless important alteration in the recruit's perception of his world orientation. Social scientists have long been aware that changes in behavior frequently effect changes in attitudes. The recruit who experiences

121

dissonance between his behavior and beliefs can effortlessly reduce his discomfort by bringing his attitudes more in line with his behavior. Few recruits want to believe that they have become unwitting pawns of the cult. To hold such a view, a recruit needs to admit to personal weakness and insincerity. Jarred by the isolation and ambiguity of their circumstances recruits are more likely to shore up their flagging self image than assail it. Consequently a recruit may distort his original orientation by placing cult needs above his own. As a result the group may take on increased value and acceptability for the recruit.

Excitement Level

Once recruits have been softened up and made responsive to the Unification perspective a subtle new tactic is added to the conversion strategy: group excitation techniques. Religious conversion, Moonies realize, requires an ardent emotional as well as intellectual commitment from recruits. For many, an intense life changing event is an essential precondition for an authentic conversion experience.

By controlling and manipulating the emotional atmosphere within the camp, Moonies can greatly increase the likelihood of a recruit experiencing a conversion. This process can best be understood within the framework of Stanley Schacter's two component theory of emotions. Schacter (1962) posits that in order for a person to experience true emotion two factors must coexist: 1) the individual must be physiologically aroused; and 2) it must be reasonable for the individual to interpret his stirred up state in emotional terms. When a person, Schacter theorizes, experiences a state of physiological arousal, for which he has no immediate explanation, he will label this state and describe his feelings in terms of the cognitions available to him. "To the extent that cognitive factors are potent determiners of emotional stress it could be anticipated that precisely the same state of physiological arousal could be labeled joy or fury or jealousy or any of a great diversity of emotional labels depending on the cognitive aspects of the situation." (Schacter p.380)

While Schacter's theory of emotions is relatively recent (1962) religious and political movements have long been aware of the benefits derived from group excitation techniques to heighten suggestibility. Rhythmic drumming which creates a state of mounting excitement among participants is found in primitive religious ceremonies throughout the world. Hitler aroused the German crowds to peaks of frenzied suggestibility through techniques such as torchlight processions and rhythmic chanting. (Sargent 1957) "The driving force of the most important changes in the world," Hitler wrote in Mein Kampf "has been found less in scientific knowledge animating the masses, but rather in fanaticism dominating them and in a hysteria which drove them forward." (p.468)

By orchestrating group activities to their advantage, Moonies can create states of intense physiological arousal in recruits while simultaneously encouraging them to interpret these stirred up feelings in religious terms. For many, the exotic environment, the ambiguous ambience of camp life, and the extensive daily regimen of activities prove strong catalysts which create considerable physiological upheaval. At strategic points along the conversion process, Moonies build upon this heightened emotional base to increase the recruits' suggestibility or possibly generate an acute religious conversion experience. By employing such emotion heightening tactics as rhythmic chanting (of Moonie slogans), or group sing alongs (using Moonie inspired lyrics to popular folk or rock songs) the membership can induce intense religious fervor. One former Moonie stated, "I think all religions...through singing, through prayer, build up a certain euphoria or a certain experience of togetherness. The [Moonies] were really good at it. There were times when I felt I was high,

123

glowing, you know; it was so sweeping, emotions were just flowing over."

The weekend is structured so that almost every activity has a function in the conversion process. Even the games are designed by Moonies to raise the emotional pitch of recruits while concurrently promoting the Unification Church message. One recruit described his first encounter with the popular Moonie game known as dodgeball during a weekend workshop.

"After lunch...we had our first session of what they call dodgeball--which was played a very specific way. You had a team in the center and a team around the outside. On each team there were certain members who were leaders and then there were certain people who were designated as shooters--and then the rest of us folks, so there were three levels of hierarchy there. Now the idea was for the team around the outside to throw the ball at the team in the middle, and if you got hit you had to leave the circle. If you could catch the ball you could give it to one of your shooters and they would try to hit somebody on the outside. If they did, one of your people got to come back to the circle. But if you caught the ball you couldn't throw it back yourself--you had to pass it to a shooter. Around the outside there were only certain people who were allowed to shoot and the rest were to try and catch the ball. It was extremely and intensely violent. People really got into it--and all the time they were chanting--like 'Win with Love' or 'Go with God', these punchy short chants. And everybody on the team was supposed to chant to try to improve your team's chances."

Throughout the workshop, cult members assist recruits in clarifying their aroused physical state in terms beneficial to the group. Should a recruit question his tumultuous reaction, Moonies are eager to provide a logical explanation: he is experiencing a profound religious conversion. Even the wary recruit, who interprets his arousal in conventional terms cannot totally ignore the potential implications of his stirred up emotions. At the very least, recruits are left shaken by the experience-- vulnerable and open to questioning their value system. Once this questioning process has been set in motion, the recruit has taken a major step toward eventual conversion.

The following schematization presents in representational terms the Unification Church's utilization of physiological arousal and interpretation.

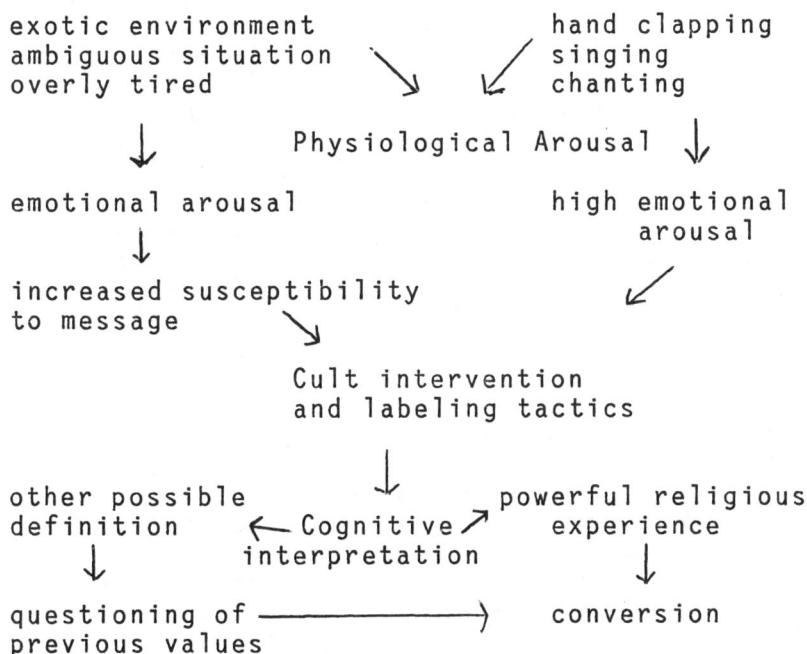

exotic environment   hand clapping
ambiguous situation   singing
overly tired   chanting

     Physiological Arousal

emotional arousal   high emotional
           arousal

increased susceptibility
to message

      Cult intervention
      and labeling tactics

other possible   powerful religious
definition   Cognitive experience
     interpretation

questioning of ⟶ conversion
previous values

125

Group Pressure

Group pressure is the most widely used and perhaps most effective method employed by the Moonies to convert recruits. Coercion tactics, both subtle and overt, are interwoven into every aspect of the weekend experience. To alter the deeply entrenched values of recruits, Moonies believe, the collective weight of the group must be brought to bear on the individual.

The psychoanalytic concept of internalization suggests that the standards of society, its rules and values, are inculcated into the child through societal representatives--the parents. Freud (1855) believed that the individual does not go through life viewing society's central norms as external and coercively imposed pressures to which he must yield. Rather, at some point in his development the individual accepts these norms as his own. These norms become internalized guidelines and the individual automatically comes to behave in accordance with them, irrespective of the presence of an external authority to enforce them.

The Unification Church's recruitment program, however, provides considerable evidence to suggest that group pressure in tandem with the previously mentioned psychological tactics create an environment ideal for the reconstruction of vulnerable individuals' normative standards. In recent years several theorists (Reiss, 1966; Wrong, 1961) have criticized the concept of internalization. They suggest that an individual's moral standards are highly vulnerable to the pressures of external forces. To be maintained these standards must be continuously supported by a pattern of social reinforcement. Reiss has proposed that the family is not the crucial agent in transmitting the values that govern the individual's adult behavior; rather, influences external to the individual assume the dominant role in directing

126

his actions. The social system, Reiss believes, may counteract the parents at any later point and reduce or replace parentally taught values. Moral norms should be defined in terms of collective behavior rather than the individual's original internalized values since internalization is not a requisite of moral behavior. Reiss cites Milgram's study of obedience as an example of people obeying an authority figure who convinced them to act against their established moral system despite the fact that they received no significant reward for doing do.

The results of Asch's experiments (1952) to determine the effect of group pressure on individual immunity to distortion led him to theorize that a person's capacity for independent action rests primarily on his relationship to himself and the others with whom he is interacting. He believes that many individuals develop an early dependency on the consensus of others and may eventually come to define themselves in terms of the evaluations others have of them. To live up to the demands of others, the "consensus dependent" individual may have to deny, ignore, or rationalize evidence of his own senses to remain consistent with the views of others. The importance of group support and approval was poignantly expressed by a former member as she recalled her years in the cult. "...respect from the other group members was worth everything. When you figure your only respect in life and sense of self esteem comes from this environment...you have only one source of self affirmation in life and that's this group. Everything else becomes meaningless."

Most recruits, Moonies realize, are attracted to the cult as a result of the interpersonal rewards and group benefits supplied by the collective membership, rather than by an acceptance (or in many cases even an understanding) of the values or beliefs espoused by the members. "Moonies," one former member reflected, "know how to make you feel good, important, like you're really something

special." Lavish praise and affection are
showered upon recruits throughout the weekend--a
technique used with awesome success by the cult
members. Even when the recruit realizes the
shallow nature of the group's affection he may
be powerless to escape its narcotic charm. One
recruit recalled an evening talent show in which
he was persuaded to perform:

> "There was real emphasis on helping you
> become more creative and more expressive.
> I noticed that I enjoyed that and took
> off some of the limitations I placed on
> myself for fear of being criticized.
> Because there was never any criticism.
> There was always lots of encouragement,
> hand clapping and applause--support and
> so on. It didn't feel entirely phony but
> you know that no one was ever going to
> get criticized no matter what they did or
> how bad it was. Nobody was going to say
> 'Oh Jesus, that was awful.'"

To understand how a recruit could be
converted into enthusiastically supporting the
goals and beliefs of a religious group with
which he disagrees or to which he is
indifferent, one must look to the theories of
Conformity, Cognitive Dissonance, and Inadequate
Justification. Conformity can be defined as a
change in a person's behavior or opinion as a
result of real or imagined pressure from a
person or group of people (Aronson, 1980, p.17).
Research, however, has indicated that conformity
that is created by the interdependence on group
consensus has two major types. One type,
compliance, refers to conformity behavior that
is not associated with the internalization of an
actual opinion change. The person publicly
behaves in a manner demanded by group pressure,
yet privately holds very different standards or
opinions. This mode of behavior is often
motivated by the complying individual's desire
to gain a reward (increased status, etc.) or
avoid punishment (social disapproval or group
isolation). Typically this behavior is only as
lasting as the promise of the reward or the
threat of punishment.

128

Internalization or conversion conformity, on the other hand, refers to an internalization of a value or belief that comes into agreement with a group as a result of a modification in the person's private belief, created by the group's influence. The motivation to internalize a particular belief is the desire to be right. Thus the reward for the belief is intrinsic. Garnier (1973) refers to this process as ideological conformity because successful adaptation is rarely exacted through systematic punishment by the group but rather generally results in the acquiring of rewards for the newly conforming individual.

Consequently a recruit's desire for approval and reconfirmation of self worth may often increase the overall attractiveness of the cult to him. That he does not particularly agree with the philosophy of the Unification Church may be of only minor importance to the flattered recruit as he basks in sensations of new found status and personal importance within the group. If the cult's attraction to the recruit rests upon its control of what the recruit wants, the group has considerable power to coerce the motivated recruit into public, but not necessarily private, conformity to its views. Recruits, then, who have begun to rely on the cult membership for the satisfaction of interpersonal needs are likely to accept publicly and even endorse the Unification philosophy--if they believe that such conformity is substantially instrumental in improving their status within the cult. Public conformity, however, does not necessarily denote private agreement. The recruit may publicly endorse the Unification principles while privately maintaining a very different set of standards. This may not be the case for long, however.

To understand how a recruit may unknowingly turn his compliance conformity to group standards into a total acceptance of the cult's norms, one must look to the theory of Cognitive Dissonance. Cognitive Dissonance (Festinger 1957) states in its most basic premise that people are compelled to maintain a consistent view of their world. In order to understand their world and cope with it people struggle to eliminate puzzling inconsistencies. dissonance occurs whenever a person holds two cognitions (ideas, attitudes, beliefs, opinions) simultaneously that are psychologically at variance with one another. For a recruit to admit that "I am publicly professing a belief in a philosophy that is incompatible with my true feelings" is likely dissonant with his belief that "I am an honest person who does not deceive people." To reduce this dissonance the recruit must change one or both cognitions in such a way as to render them consonant. Dissonance theory, however, does not picture people as rational beings, rather, it pictures them as rationalizing beings--particularly when their self concept is threatened. According to an underlying assumption of the theory "people are motivated not so much to be right--rather, they are motivated to believe that they are right." (Aronson p.95) Dissonance reducing behavior is often ego defensive behavior in that "by reducing dissonance we maintain a positive image of ourselves--an image that depicts us as good or smart or worthwhile." (Aronson p.95)

Festinger and Carlsmith (1959) studied situations in which dissonance was created when a person says something or behaves in a manner that he does not believe. Referred to as the theory of Inadequate Justification the authors postulate that the fewer the external justifications available to a person behaving in a manner inconsistent with his private beliefs, the greater is the likelihood that he will reduce his dissonance by changing his private beliefs to become consistent with his public behavior. In other words, an individual who has conformed in the face of group compliance pressure may decide that his original, underlying attitudes were in fact consistent with his public behavior. He therefore eliminates any dissonance between his actual behavior and his internal attitudes and beliefs. This formulation is based on the assumption that most people like to think of themselves as honest, decent individuals who wouldn't ordinarily mislead others without just cause. Therefore if the compliant recruit makes several public statements of support for the group's philosophy that he cannot justify externally (such as "I was paid to say those things") he will attempt to justify it internally by making his attitudes more consistent with his statements. The recruit is not changing his beliefs because of any reward (compliance), he is changing his attitudes because he has succeeded in convincing himself that his previous attitudes were incorrect (conversion). This, as Aronson (1980) observes, is a very powerful form of attitude change. The previously compliant conforming recruit, through a desire for cognitive consistency, abandons his former basis for making interpretations of the importance of the group's goals and philosophies and is converted to the ideology of the Unification Church.

TYPOLOGIES

One of the oldest endeavors of psychology is to develop a useful typology to express in some simplified form the diversity of character among humans.

The following chapters are an attempt to define the salient personality characteristics that render certain young people susceptible to the ministrations and conversion techniques practiced by the Unification Church.

One should recognize that these typologies represent ideal models into which no one individual is likely to fit neatly. Further, the models are neither all inclusive nor totally indicative of the range of personality characteristics associated with individuals who are attracted to the Unification Church.

Each Moonie and former Moonie interviewed was unique in his or her reasons for becoming a member of the Unification Church and can only be understood within the context of his or her entire personality makeup.

CHAPTER XV

IMMATURE EMOTIONAL

"It seemed strange, that here were six people all looking alike, with the same gestures and all of them saying the same things."

> — a mother of a Moonie discussing her daughter's cult friends

"By watching my older sister and brother--and the older people on my block, I said — Well, I think I'll wait. There's nothing out there yet."

> — a 22 year old Moonie

Erik Erikson (1958) refers to adolescence as a particularly troublesome transition period in the development of the personality. Each young person, at this stage, Erikson observed, must develop "some central perspectives and directions, some working unity out of the effective remnants of his anticipated adulthood." (p.14) Perplexed by the baffling array of contrasting values and role models, young people often become alarmed by the unexpected complexity of their lives. The impending responsibilities of adulthood and concerns about their future livelihood are of considerable importance to youth as they approach maturity.

"At the point that I met the
Unification Church," a young female
Moonie relates, "I was really searching -
seeking what was my purpose in life.
What was the direction I was going in.
Because at this point, I was 19 years old
- I didn't have an education. I didn't
have any really solid ground in my life.
I was really looking to my future. What
do I have for a future - I didn't have
anything."

Lacking a well developed identity and ego
ideal, young people often project their feelings
of self-doubt and confusion onto a safer, less
personal target - the world. In their fearful
eyes the world is unstable; society is seen as
muddled, in clear need of standards or
direction.

Unnerved by the intensity of their
anxiety, some frightened youth may wish to
return to the safe uncluttered world of their
childhood. Life, they recall, was simple then;
demands were few, needs were satisfied, and they
were not responsible for making life changing
decisions. "Man has two faces," Meerlo (1961)
noted, "he wants to grow toward maturity and
freedom and yet the primitive child in his
unconscious yearns for complete protection and
irresponsibility." (p.107)

For the security conscious youth, a
totalitarian environment (like that of the
Unification Church) provides an ideal escape
route from the world of responsibility.
Abdication of the decision making process
renders temporarily a giddy sense of peace.
Simply to feel loved and protected is the
motivational intent of these young people.

The Immature Emotional's overwhelming
hunger for security and the resultant childlike
submission to authority appears to take on two
distinct, major forms among Unification Church
members: 1) The Authority Seeker and 2) the
Simple Answer Seeker. While similar in
underlying motivation the Authority Seeker and

134

Simple Answer Seeker are unique in critical
respects. Therefore I have assigned a separate
chapter to each.

CHAPTER XVI

THE AUTHORITY SEEKER

"It wasn't that I was looking for some
sanctuary, some security but there was security
there [in the movement]. And there was love and
it was genuine love; it wasn't just a game."

- a 23 year old Moonie

"If you had any sense at all of not being
loved or doubting yourself or needing external
support, they [Moonies] would jump right in the
middle of that and give you all kinds of
encouragement and love and so forth. That way
they would establish a dependency relationship
on the group, substituting in many ways for
anyone outside the group like parents,
boyfriends, girlfriends. All your need for
affection, affiliation and group support would
get focused on being a member of the group."

- a 26 year old former Moonie

The authority seeker is a young person
drawn to the Unification Church by a desire to
find parent replacements--people who will love
and protect him like his biological parents.

This unconscious search for parent
surrogates can best be understood by examining
the process of authority transference. This
psychoanalytic concept states that the formative

roots of later attitudes toward authority can be
traced back to the early attitudes toward
parental authority.

Faced with the decisions of approaching
adulthood, some ego diffused young people may
wish to avoid the responsibilities of maturity
by retreating back to the less complex
behavioral standards of childhood. As a result
they are attracted to relationships with
authority figures which resemble their earlier
interactions with their parents. These
associations frequently take on the character of
domination (parent role) and submission (child
role) that the individual found so comforting as
a youngster. It is not unusual for authority
figures to become identified as parent
replacements in the youth's mind--individuals
that he defers to and idealizes similar to his
parents.

Underlying the authority transference
theory are the psychoanalytic concepts of
identification and introjection. It becomes
relatively simple for the emotionally regressed
youth to project the omnipotent characteristics
of his childish parental perceptions onto an
authority figure (in this case Reverend Moon or
his surrogate).

It is no coincidence that the membership
address Reverend Moon as "Father" or refer to
the cult as "the family." Studies have
suggested that special words which have high
emotional content (such as Father or family)
tend to influence people into an automatic
manner of thinking related to those words.
Meerlo, (1961) for example, observed that some
words "are conditioners, emotional triggers,
serving to imprint the desired reaction patterns
on their hearts." (p.136)

The frequent exploitation of emotion
laden words serve to define and maintain the
authority structure between leaders and
followers in the cult. Semantic distinctions
are subtly drawn within the Church hierarchy.
Father is a title specifically reserved for

Reverend Moon while the sobriquet "Minister"
(followed by the individual's surname) is
employed by subordinates when addressing or
referring to the Church elite. The
characterization of Reverend Moon as "Father"
establishes the correct mind set among members
for the development of a favorable identity
association with him--an association based upon
pleasant, past parental memories. In addition
the "Father" designation enhances the likelihood
that young people will project their feelings
and ideals held about their biological parents
onto him. The "Minister" specification confers
status upon loyal and competent underlings and
establishes clear lines of authority among the
membership. Similarly the label "family" when
alluding to the cult fosters a favorable
emotional climate among the membership. For
most people the word "family" holds the promise
of intense personal relationships with people
who will provide unquestioning love and support.

Through the process of labeling and
authority transference, some recruits (and
members) may come to assume that the authority
structure of the cult reflects that of their
biological family. They may naively expect that
the cult authority will be as benign and
democratic as their original family structure.
There are, however, some essential differences
in the theoretical makeup of the two groups.
The family is based upon the relationship
between the parent and child, and on the need of
the child for care and security. The
relationship is bonded together by mutual
affection. The cult, on the other hand, while
promoting the impression of care and protection,
is primarily based on cooperation to provide for
the necessities of life. While affection alone
can maintain the unity of the family, the cult
must subordinate affection to the common
interests and goals of the group.

"It is not at all a family," one
disgruntled former member recalled. "It
is very much of a hierarchical system.
In the Unification Church, people are not
equal at all--not brothers and sisters.

You have people on pedestals and people down in the dirt--peons."

Authority transference and the resulting childlike dependence and regression pattern employed (unconsciously) by some young people to avoid the impending responsibilities of adulthood, can have a damaging impact on those who assume this role within the cult. Not only their behavior, but also their biological functioning may revert to more immature standards. Dramatic loss of facial hair in males and the alteration of menses in females have been noted by cult researchers (Clark, 1979). One mother described the startling changes that were appearing in her newly converted daughter's correspondence from a Moonie center in California:

> "In the course of writing we [her husband and herself] saw something that was very disturbing to us. Her handwriting changed. Her verbal communication--her method of communication--changed, became much more simplistic. Her vocabulary seemed to have shrunk. She was using only the most simple expressions. She was drawing pictures. She was relying on pictures. She would talk about something she was very happy about and she would draw the happy face. Or she would say something that happened--she got caught in the rain--she would draw the sad face. This disturbed us very much because this was not like her."

For the youth caught in an unending spiral of authority transference, the cult leader (or his surrogate) assumes the role of parent figure to be obeyed unquestionably. The youth relates to this authority figure in a manner similar to his relationships with his biological parents during the stage of delegated omnipotence. One recruit (a Ph.'D. candidate at the time) referred to a female Church member, several years his junior as "my spiritual mommy." He unknowingly conveyed the depth of his authority transference in a discussion

140

regarding his desire to leave the Moonie training camp in Boonesville California.

> "It was all psychological pressure--it wasn't physical restraint. I wasn't going to walk away and leave her. I wanted her permission...that she was going to say it was all right. We talked about it for 3 days and finally she said that she trusted me implicitly. So I said, 'If you really trust me, let me go, because that's what I think I should do.'"

Willing subjugation to a totalitarian ideology cannot be understood completely as a desire to return to a safe childhood pattern of interaction with parent figures. Psychologists such as Freud, Rogers, Sullivan, and Piaget have all recognized the importance of childhood experience in the formation of adult attitudes toward authority. They agree that attitudes toward authority originate in the child's family structure with his powerful parents and are later generalized as attitudes toward authority figures in subsequent interactions. When the family socialization standard inculcates the child with deferential attitudes toward authority, the developing youth may internalize these submissive values.

Theorists have expanded Freud's illumination of the profound impact of the nuclear family structure on the formation of attitudes toward authority to include the importance of institutions in the socialization process. Friedenberg, (1965) for example, argues that the power exercised by school authority figures, ostensibly to maintain order, may have unanticipated consequences of usurping student initiative and limiting their capacity for independent judgments. Schools, Friedenberg points out, are designed to a large degree to socialize and instill compliant attitudes toward authority figures so as to ensure the effective operation of the organization. The fundamental method of control in almost every school is based on the model of authority domination and student submission. Blay (1965) observed a similar pattern in employment organizations; "The combined effect of bureaucracy's characteristics is to create social conditions which constrain each member of the organization to act in ways that, whether they appear rational or otherwise from his individual standpoint, further the rational pursuit of organizational objectives." (p.48)

Consequently, some young people may grow up accepting their submissive roles as appropriate, failing to question values or decisions when commanded by an authority figure.

> "There is no way," explained a former Moonie about his emotional decision to join the group, "that you can go to a Catholic school for eight years and not develop a respect for authority. People are really trained to go along with things in a Catholic high school."

The study on obedience conducted at Yale University in the mid 1960s demonstrates the extent to which obedience toward authority is embedded in the American adult's character structure. The experiment focused on the amount of electric shock a subject is willing to administer to another person when ordered by an experimenter to give the victim increasingly higher wattage of shock. The majority of almost one thousand adult subjects, individually observed in the research, delegated the process of judgement for the safety of their fellow subjects to the unknown experimenter. They performed acts of perceived brutality that were termed "callous" and "severe" by the experimenters. The experiment designer, Stanley Milgram (1973), concluded: "The results as seen and felt in the laboratory are to this author disturbing. They raise the possibility that human nature or--more specifically--the kind of character produced in American democratic society, cannot be counted on to insulate its citizens from brutality and inhumane treatment at the direction of malevolent authority. A substantial portion of people do what they are told to do irrespective of the content of the act and without limitations of conscience, so long as they perceive that the command comes from a legitimate authority." (p.37)

Unification recruiters exploit conforming young people's predisposition to obey authority to great advantage throughout the recruitment process. For example, recruiters frequently press recalcitrant target individuals into making hasty commitments to group activities by failing to provide them with an alternative. Caught off guard, the target may perceive an emphatic invitation to a group activity to be an order. Startled by the intensity of the request some young people may comply, not out of interest, but as a reflex response toward authority.

For the youth whose capacity for independent judgement remains underdeveloped, Moonie cult life may prove idyllic. Delegating his capacity for moral evaluation to the group (or its policy makers) relieves the uncertain convert of the burden of responsibility for improper personal decisions.

To abrogate one's judgement is not without cost, however, as Asch (1952) observed. "To be independent is to assert the authentic value of one's experience; to yield is to deny the evidence on one's senses, to permit oneself to become confused about one's experience, to suppress evidence that cannot be assimilated--to renounce a condition which one's capacity to function depends on in an essential way." (p.86)

CHAPTER XVII

THE SIMPLE ANSWER SEEKER

"I was not an intellectual person. I was a people person. If I like the way the people felt, the energy I got from them, the way they responded to me, how much they gave or how much they really showed the true side of themselves-- then I say I'll stick with that."

                    - a 22 year old Moonie

"We are all young. We are all healthy. We are all well educated--in the organization. It is easy to believe that we are the progenitors of the heavenly kingdom."

                    - a 26 year old former Moonie

The Simple Answer Seeker (S.A.S) is a young person struggling with the complexity of his emerging adult identity. Unsure of his own questionable decision making ability, the S.A.S. reduces his discomfort through the assimilation of a cognitive framework and membership pattern in a group that promises an all inclusive, meaningful interpretation of life. He links his own weakly established identity with that of movement hoping to find purpose in his life and protection from the insecurities of adult decision making.

By embracing an all encompassing, simple solution to life's problems the S.A.S. convincingly denies the growing complexity in

his life. Unlike the mature idealist the S.A.S.
strives to escape from the responsibilities of a
complex world rather than face the challenge
directly. He desperately wants to believe that
Nirvana is possible; that lasting happiness is
within his grasp. "It's a real childlike kind
of innocence," related one female, former
member. "It's a ten-year-old's perspective:
'God and my leader are going to take care of me
and everything is secure and there is an answer
for everything.'"

Moonies are all too eager to reinforce
the myth of perpetual bliss through the mere
acceptance of their doctrine. While out
recruiting, their calm, smiling countenance
frequently presents a striking counterpoint to
the grim expression of society at large.
Moonies outward enthusiasm and blissful visage
is not lost on some youthful cult observers.
They assume, quite naturally from the joyful
presence of the recruiter that he must possess a
formula for happiness. A constantly cheerful
demeanor, however, can also create scorn and
suspicion in a society unused to such exuberant
emotional displays. Many wary society members
assume that anyone this happy must be
brainwashed.

Youth, by it's very nature, fervently
seeks out man and ideas to have faith in.
Erikson (1968) observed, "It is the ideological
potential of society that speaks most clearly to
the adolescent who is eager to be affirmed by
peers, to be confirmed by teachers and to be
inspired by worthwhile ways of life. (p.130)
But in today's complex American society, young
people are faced with a proliferation of diverse
and frequently incompatible choices for models
and ideals. The freedom to choose among these
diverse models further complicates the
adolescent's construction of a stable, coherent
identity. "Youth," Toffler (1970) notes, "may
well be the victims of the dilemma of
overchoice." (p.241)

The Moonie lifestyle may be viewed by
some youth as an attractive refuge from this

fearful and confusing reality. The cult
provides a sanctuary - a respite from decisions.
The Divine Principle furnishes the young person
with an already existing foundation of values,
ideals, principles and behavioral guidelines.
By merging his identity with the movement, doubt
is replaced by certainty; insecurity is
supplanted by confidence. The new convert
experiences an exhilarating rush of freedom and
power. He need no longer worry about developing
outside interests, talents or relationships
which are not directly associated with the
movement's goals. By dedicating his whole
energy to the ideals of the Church all outside
considerations, with their inherent potential
for failure, are avoided. Everything, a
frightened convert may rationalize, pales in
significance to the critical mission of the
Church. The idealistic tenor of the doctrine
provides a practical smokescreen for the S.A.S.
to convince both himself and others of his
competency level as a person. By submerging his
personal identity into the idealistic aspects of
the group's doctrine, the youthful convert can
maintain a cognitively consistent perception of
himself as a dedicated, capable person while
simultaneously avoiding the consequences
attached to independent thinking.

No matter how attractive the initial
inducements are to the S.A.S. recruit, one would
expect that commitment to the cult would
eventually depend on the group's ability to
articulate a convincing truth. S.A.S. recruits,
however, may need less convincing than other
potential members. They want to believe that a
magic formula exists to eradicate world and
personal problems. They are highly motivated to
accept less than the dramatic results they were
originally promised. In their determined quest
for internal relief, S.A.S. recruits may alter
their reality to become consistent with their
fantasies. For their part, cult members
circumvent disappointed reactions to inflated
expectations (created by zealous recruitment) by
stressing to eager adherents that the fruits of
their experiences will be discovered in
increasing degrees as the novice grows toward

147

spiritual maturity. Thus while the recruit
awaits the revelation of truth, the cult has an
opportunity to increase his commitment potential
through more indirect methods.

CHAPTER XVIII

THE IDEALS SEEKER

"Holding hands--kinda nice, low level
sexual pleasure. To be close to people, touch
people, look at them eye to eye without some
contact or compromising overtones."

                    - a 25 year old former Moonie

"For these kids everything is black and
white in a world that is gray."

                    - a parent of a high ranking
                      Moonie

A second typology of youth who are rooted
in an identity struggle, and particularly
susceptible to the Unification Church influence,
is the Ideals Seeker. The Ideals Seeker is a
young person who clings tenaciously to an
outmoded sense of childhood morality in an
attempt to avoid the anxiety resulting from his
identity confusion.

Youth is normally a time of great
ideological receptivity when each person
searches for a new order and meaning in his
life. Rebellion against the established social
order (parents, society, etc.) is a familiar
gesture of each generation of youth. Erikson
(1968) believes that adolescents need to explore
a diversity of alternatives along their path
toward preparation for adult autonomy. During
this searching period, the previously trusted

institutions of parents and society come under
scrutiny by youthful interpreters. The failings
and hypocrisies of the previous generation
create considerable conflict for the rigidly
idealistic youth. Measured against the strict
moral standards of adolescence, both adults and
their society are frequently found wanting.
Youths' natural idealism and their resulting
cynicism with the flawed values of society
generally evolve over time into the realism of
maturity.

For some young people, however, idealism
becomes a crutch for avoiding the impending
responsibilities and roles of adulthood. It
provides fearful youths with a cognitively
acceptable vehicle for subordinating the
anxieties related to their identity crisis. For
these young people the idealistic message of the
Unification Church has high appeal. This
concept of a wholesome world free of selfish
interests is poignantly expressed by a young
Unification Church member:

"The whole idea, the whole basic
understanding is if we can really come to
practice the love of the Christian ideal
the whole world could be so
different...The Christian love would just
be radiant in all society. We wouldn't
have any problems with poverty. The
people that were rich would have such a
heart when they see somebody suffering
they would give him money to help out--
even give him a job--anything."

For most youth, successful growth into a
competent adult depends, to a large extent, on
their ability to meet new needs and expand their
identities to accommodate challenging new
situations. The Ideals Seeker, however,
attempts to deny his growing awareness of the
complexity of his human nature and that of the
world at large. By clinging to a strict,
childhood morality, he takes refuge in an
ethical system which provides an acceptable
mechanism to avoid threatening new feelings.

For many young people the period of emerging sexuality can be very difficult. The adjustments created by this exciting yet threatening new aspect of their identity can be very disorienting. New drives and desires make it difficult for the inexperienced young person to relate to peers (particularly those of the opposite sex) in a comfortable way. Most young people eventually adjust to the new emotions created by their sexual awakening. Some youths, however, attempt to circumvent the trauma involved in resolving their emerging sexuality by seeking out a safe alternative.

The Ideals Seeker regresses back to the safety of his childhood morality system which provides him with an acceptable justification for the denial of his erotic feelings. By finding that the solution to his fears about sexuality lies in adherence to a strict idealistic framework, the frightened youth effectively reduces the anxiety associated with developing individual moral standards. The Unification Church's strict adherence to a moral structure which condemns overt expressions of sexuality between unmarried members creates a tension free environment, attractive to the Ideals Seeker. He can interact comfortably with the members in a consciously non-sexual manner. He need not fear that the cult membership will verbally or behaviorally compromise his childlike sexual standards.

"One thing for me that was great," observed a male former member, "was the physical support of the group. The handholding, the backrubs were uncomfortable at first, but it was nice being able to hug. There is trust at that level--it takes a complex, complicated factor out of your life--sexuality." A female Moonie takes a somewhat different perspective. She commented, "I could have real relationships with people, honest relationships based on character and personality and not on my body or what we could do for each other physically."

Young peoples' attraction toward an idealistic movement or idealized person may be a

151

result of other factors associated with the
identity crisis. Knight (1968) theorizes that
the psychological origins of youths' attraction
to religiosocial idealism stems, to some extent,
from their desperate yearning for peace and
tranquility within themselves. By projecting
their own feelings of inner turmoil and
confusion onto the outside world, Knight
suggests, the idealistic young are merely
transforming their own longing for inner peace
into a more acceptable wish for world peace.
They simply project their internal turmoil
outward by actively seeking resolution to world
problems. In so doing, youthful idealists have
a concrete and less personally threatening
method of dealing with their identity formation.

Winder (1968) postulates that some
youths' commitment to an idealized person is
more a result of unmet needs than ideological
interest. He suggests that an idealized person
helps the floundering young person relieve the
anxiety which accompanies increased independence
from their parents. This idealized person,
Winder observes, "is a substitute to fill the
void, a substitute who is uncontaminated by the
incestful wishes and guilt that were part of the
child's relationship with his parents."

Regaining the feeling of childhood
security may be particularly important to some
college students. Sheltered and protected
throughout their childhood and adolescence, many
first-year college students are handed over
complete responsibility for their lives all at
once. Freshmen may find the independence of
college stressful. Not only must they deal with
the anxiety of parental separation, but they are
also expected to make mature career and life
choices. Forced to rely on their own seldom
used decision making process, some students
panic. They seek out an idealized adult and
adopt his ideology. In so doing, the frightened
young person not only establishes a fixed point
on which to orient his values but also regains a
sense of parental security.

152

The following facets of life in the
Unification Church attract the Ideals Seeker and
may encourage him to become an active
participant in the cult:

- A Father Figure

The movement presents the image of an
idealized person (Reverend Moon) to serve as a
parent surrogate.

- A Philosophy

The cult provides the Ideals Seeker with
a rigid philosophical structure. This structure
is complete with simplistic absolutes on the
meaning of life and the reason for human
existence. By following these guidelines
members believe they will achieve happiness and
spiritual perfection.

- Spiritual Perfection

The cult expresses a commitment to
enhance the followers' spiritual development.
Cult members are totally dedicated to a way of
life which lends their activities sacred
significance.

- Unambiguous Moral Standards

The Unification Church maintains strict
moral standards for group members' sexual
behavior. Rigid adherence to the cult's moral
standards eliminates any anxiety associated with
sexual feelings surfacing in the group.

- Social Contributions

Members believe that they make
significant contributions towards the
advancement of social justice, world peace, and

unity among man through their commitment to cult
sponsored activities.

   - Peer Solidarity

    The cult takes advantage of young
people's natural cynicism toward preceding
generations. By subtly attacking the
hypocrisies of parents, religious and social
figures, and thus establishing a common enemy,
Moonies generate increased ideological
identification among idealistic youth.

    In addition, members receive huge amounts
of peer affirmation to offset the anxiety
created by the recruits' separation from home
and family.

   - Rituals

    The movement practices numerous rituals
and ceremonies and exudes a rich sense of
tradition. This aspect of cult life is
exhilarating yet comforting for group members.

CHAPTER XIX

THE SOCIAL NON-CONFORMIST

"If you see your child involved with
dope, sleeping around with married women--going
around and all of a sudden he comes home clean
cut Johnny--apple pie, hair cut, suit, even lost
a couple of pounds...Mom says, 'Oh-oh, this
ain't right.' She can't accept the fact that
God can do something."

- a 22 year old Moonie

"Six months into the organization, I knew
that there was no way that I was going to tell
them I'm gay. It would have destroyed my career
with the Church. I know that if you said really
bad stuff you'd be doomed. There was nothing to
be gained about being honest about seamy stuff."

- a 25 year old former Moonie

The third typology of youth which become
attracted to the Unification Church is referred
to as the social non-conformist. The social
non-conformist is an individual who is unwilling
or unable to adapt successfully to the
prevailing norms of society and thus seeks out a
group or social environment that provides norms
to which he can conform.

Conforming behavior has been defined as
"behavior reflecting the successful influence of
other persons." (Stinchcombe, 1964, p. 34)
Aronson (1980) has suggested two possible

155

reasons why an individual might conform. One is that the behaviors of others might convince us that our original judgement was wrong. The other is that a person may wish to avoid punishment (such as rejection or ridicule) or gain a reward (such as acceptance or approval) from a group.

Deviant behavior, on the other hand, has often been viewed as the flip side of conformity or behavior reflecting the rejected influence of others. (Stinchcombe, 1964)

For the social non-conformist however, his attraction to the Unification Church arises not from the rejected influence of others, nor from a reformulation of ideology, but develops from the identical wellsprings of motivation as conformity. His is a failure to meet societal standards which he comes to perceive as rejection from society.

In many cases, the price for deviant adaptation to societal standards in America is to suffer its most harsh sanction--emotional alienation. By collectively withholding acceptance and approval from those individuals who violate the prevailing norms, society successfully enforces its standards while ensuring a minimum amount of non-conformist expression. Potent and often very subtle mechanisms are constantly applied to actual or potential non-conformists. Persuasion, ridicule, gossip, or undermining of status are brought to bear on a non-conforming individual to reshape his behavior in accordance with the accepted rules, standards, and expectations of society. A direct challenge to our cultural norms or values often leads to an immediate reduction in status for the offending individual and castigation by conforming members of society.

Numerous studies have shown that most people are likely to accept, and even endorse, demands for conformity, if conformity is seen as substantially instrumental in increasing their status or gaining acceptance and approval. In

156

other words, people are likely to conform to standards if they believe that deviation will result in the undermining of their status or the loss of a valued job or object.

Nevertheless, some individuals are unwilling or unable to accept the standards and attitudes of normative society. As Flacks (1963) points out "standards may be such that he (the deviant) lacks the requisite skills, talents or resources to perform adequately. In some cases the very act of attempting to conform may have implications for the person which he simply cannot afford. He is faced with a situation in which he must undergo important change in order to maintain himself in the group or else face some significant degree of social disapproval or loss of status." (p. 8)

If one accepts the assumption that rejection by a valued group (in this case society) elicits feelings of hostility toward the rejecting group, then the resultant anger can be dealt with in two basic ways.

One is that the individual may turn his hostility outward, toward the group, exhibiting rebellious and non-conformist behavior. Several theorists (Stinchcombe, 1964; Keniston, 1968; Erikson, 1968) have proposed that the strain between internalized standards of success and the inaccessibility of reaching those norms frequently produces rebellion. In the second case, the individual may turn his hostility inward, onto himself creating a strong need for reassurance. This is the group of individuals who comprise the category referred to here as social non-conformers. Obviously, the greater the extent to which the individual turns society's rejection inward, the greater the likelihood is that the rejection will cause a lowering of self-esteem and create a potential threat to the person's self-image. We are all motivated to believe that we are right and good and decent. (Aronson, 1980)

In achievement oriented societies, such as the United States, the threat to a non-

conformist self-image may be particularly
severe. When the prevailing cultural norms
state that opportunities are equal for everyone
and that status is the result of performance,
then one's ranking in society provides some
tangible evidence of an individual's competence
and worth. So if an individual's rank in
society is low (as is the case for many non-
conformists) the most plausible assumption is
that his performance and/or abilities may be
inferior to those of others.

Consequently, the rejected individual who
turns his hostility inward is faced with three
basic alternatives:

1) He may continue to maintain his
current pattern of behavior and face
significant social disapproval, loss of
status and esteem.

2) He may attempt to undergo critical
changes in his behavior patterns in order
to become more consistent with normative
society and thus raise his status and
acceptability.

3) He may seek out a social environment
that has norms to which he can conform,
while simultaneously reducing his
dependence for acceptance and status on
normative society.

When an individual turns society's
rejection inward, he must somehow reconcile this
fact with his view of himself and his
performance.

Initially, he may strive to gain social
reassurance by attempting to conform to
society's influence irrespective of whether it
fits his preferred style of living. A study by
Festinger, Schacter and Beck (1950) concluded
that the more an individual values membership in
a particular group, the more he will conform to
the group's demands.

If, however, acceptance is not forthcoming or the imposed societal norms and standards place unrealistic demands on the non-conformist, he will likely do three things to maintain his self-image.

1) Attempt to invalidate the negative evaluation of the group through the accumulation of real or rationalized evidence.

2) Make society and its norms a less attractive group and rationalize a decrease of desire for acceptance and status within it.

3) Seek out others whose judgement of his behavior is not negative and place value on their opinion.

By returning to the theory of cognitive dissonance (Festinger, 1957) this phenomenon can be better understood. One need remember that an underlying concept of dissonance theory states that people are compelled to maintain a consistent view of their world and they endeavor to remove contradictions between any two simultaneously held cognitions. To hold two ideas such as "Society is the best judge of individual worth" and "Society holds me in very low esteem" or "I am an intelligent person who makes sensible decisions" and "The great majority of people think I am making incorrect judgments" are incompatible and threatening to a person's self-image. To reduce the apparent dissonance, an individual must change one or both cognitions in such as way as to render the two ideas consonant.

Through a series of rationalizations, the social non-conformist can reduce his dissonance over his failure to be accepted by society. By invalidating society's ability to judge individual worth and simultaneously downgrading the attractiveness of accepted membership, the non-conformist can maintain cognitive consistency while retaining a positive self-image.

The desire for social approval and status often provides the initial impetus for the attraction to deviant subgroups. If one cannot behave in accordance with the prevailing standards and norms of society, it is logical to seek out a subgroup where the criteria for acceptance and status can be achieved by the non-conforming individual. The key feature of a deviant subculture, according to Flacks (1963), is the collective "development of counter-norms and counter criteria for status within the larger system." (p.19) Consequently the non-conforming participants can achieve a level of status not accorded them in society while simultaneously rejecting the standards established and maintained by a society which frustrates them.

The need for approval, acceptability, and status has been well documented in the literature. The positive relationship between deviance and status needs is found in studies of group dynamics (Festinger, Schacter, Back, 1950). Atkinson (1958) labeled it the affiliation motive and noted that humans have a powerful need for social acceptance by others. He characterized people as striving to attain the satisfaction which accompanies the establishment of warm, affectionate relationships with others. For an individual who has been repeatedly rejected by normative society, membership in a cohesive group, even a deviant subculture, fulfills many of his affiliation needs and constitutes a direct proof of his worth. "For me," one male, former Moonie explained, "it was the chance to fit in." Later, in the same interview, he characterized himself in the following way: "I've always been sort of a loner. I think very well respected, but not a chummy sort of person. I was very much that way in college...I was a puritanical activist. The image I had with my friends and housemates was a monastic sort of person."

In order to understand the social non-conformist attraction to the Unification Church, one needs to re-examine the previously stated methods for maintaining self-esteem in light of

160

the Unification Church's potential philosophic and social benefits.

1) The non-conformist will attempt to invalidate the negative evaluation of the group (society) through the accumulation of real or rationalized evidence.

The Moonie philosophy provides the social non-conformist with a cognitively acceptable rationale for explaining society's low opinion of him. Acceptance into the cult, the deviant is informed, results from a capacity for spiritual superiority - a precious gift from God. Moonies, converts believe, are modern day social martyrs with the insight, courage and stamina to pursue their religious ideals. The membership's collective confidence in their movement's eventual vindication from outside critics is reflected in a popular Unification poster: "Skeptics and cynics mocked and persecuted religious leaders of the past such as Moses and Jesus. History proved their detractors lacked vision and acted in ignorance of the truth." By transforming society's substandard evaluation of him into a virtuous search for religious truth, the social non-conformist can regain a feeling of self regard.

2) The non-conformist will make society and its norms a less attractive group and rationalize a decrease of desire for acceptance and status within it.

Moonies are repelled by the sin and corruption they see existing within the satanically dominated framework of normative society. Convinced of the inescapable corruption of a devil influenced society, followers naturally spurn its value and status system. In its place, members have constructed their own elaborate value and status order replete with a convincing rationale for its superiority over society's sinful structure.

161

By accepting the Moonie perspective and renouncing society's values as devil dominated, the non-conformist can conveniently reduce his desire for acceptance and status outside the cult. Failure to adapt to a satanically influenced society, the non-conformist may reason, results not from weakness but rather spiritual fortitude.

3) The social non-conformist may seek out others whose judgement of his behavior is not negative and place value of their opinions.

As individuals, most Moonies can empathize with the friendless, the ostracized or the outcasts from normative society. Products themselves of overwhelming social disapproval for their irregular religious beliefs, cult members daily experience the sting of massive societal rejection. As a result, they realize that a non-judgmental attitude when combined with the opportunity for warmth and friendship can be a devastatingly successful method of appealing to the lonely.

Moonies are rarely critical of a non-conforming recruit's limitations or failures. They are quick to sympathize with his problems and eager to boost his morale through flattery. If society represents failure and rejection to the non-conformist, the Church symbolizes status and belonging. Recognition, love, and concern are powerful lures to the non-conformist, as one former member explained.

"A lot of it (joining the Moonies) had to do with fitting in; I had this great energy--this great sense of mission and this great sense of alienation--that I didn't fit into the rock music scene. I didn't fit into college. I wasn't into the team sport thing. I mean I was a loner and I didn't know all the jargon-- you know, rapping about things. I was stiff. In a sense I fit in with that here. There was a mission--there was a

purpose--there was the sense of you
(being) the most important person in the
world. That's how I felt about myself.
Also, there was stereotyped language. We
dressed the same - we ate the same - we
talked the same. There was always
something to talk about because there
wasn't much to talk about. What's your
mission? How are you doing? A small
vocabulary really."

Moonies are caught up in a common destiny
and share an intense collective identity. They
understand one another's problems - particularly
the isolation born out of an unpopular
perspective. Warmth and support among members
(both genuine and feigned) gives each Moonie
courage to continue his difficult mission. No
member goes unnoticed. For the non-conformist
this may be reason enough to belong.

"At least you are always with someone,"
one former member related. "They always
know where you are. They miss you. If
you get depressed or something like that,
they may come at you with a strange point
of view - like you aren't going to be
able to perform - or you're not going to
be able to accomplish your mission - but
they notice and they are right there.
There is a lot of support."

METHOD

CHAPTER XX

METHOD

Subjects

A total of thirty-eight individuals
participated in the study on either a formal or
informal basis. These subjects can be divided
logically into three major classifications.

1) Current members of the Unification
Church

2) Former members of the Unification
Church

3) Parents of current or former members
of the Unification Church

Current Members

The primary focus of the study centered
around interviewing, observing and interacting
with Moonies. Twenty-eight current members of
the Unification Church including the group's
student wing known as Carp, participated in the
study. Eight members were interviewed formally,
employing a preconceived set of interview
questions which were taped and later reviewed at
length. The remaining twenty members were
interviewed informally over the course of my
association with them while conducting the
study. Informal interviews were characterized
by unstructured (often spontaneous) non-taped

166

discussions arising out of questions, concerns, issues or perspectives affecting either the responding member or the Unification Church.

The study's participants were comprised of Church members from the Ann Arbor, Detroit, Lansing and Columbus centers. In addition, an advisor to Carp centers whose home base is located in New York City also agreed to take part in the study.

The subjects' ages ranged between nineteen and thirty-six years. The length of individual membership in the Unification Church varied from eleven months to twelve years. Eighteen males and ten females, including Caucasians, Blacks and Orientals engaged in the project.

Former Members

Four former members of the Unification Church participated in the study. In addition, one individual was interviewed who declined official membership in the group yet attended several Church organized recruitment activities (including the dinner meeting, the weekend workshop and two week long workshops).

At the time of their interviews, four of the five participants of this subgroup were enrolled in undergraduate or graduate courses at the University of Michigan. Their ages ranged between twenty-three and thirty-five years. Their length of membership in the Unification Church varied from one month to five years with an overall group average of over two years. Three of the four former members were actively involved in the Unification Church for over three years. The participants were all Caucasian and male with the exception of one female.

Parents of Current or Former Members

Personal interviews were conducted with the parents of two former and one current member of the Unification Church. A total of five parents (three mothers and two fathers) were involved in the study. A husband and wife set comprised two of the three interview sessions. The five parents were all Caucasian, upper middle class, Detroit area residents.

In two cases, the son or daughter involved with the cult (both former members) were interviewed separately in another section of the study. Neither the parents nor the offspring were aware of the content of the other's interview. All participants involved willingly agreed to this format prior to the interview schedule.

All five parents belong to a loosely structured anti-cult parent organization. The goals of this organization are numerous and varied. Their most important functions include 1) acting as a support system for parents whose children are involved with cults, 2) monitoring the overt activities of several cults, 3) providing information to the public regarding their perception of the destructive nature of several cults.

Individual interviews were conducted at a variety of locations during the summer and fall of 1980, and the winter of 1981. Unification Church members were interviewed under diverse circumstances at a variety of locations. Formal interviews with Moonies were conducted exclusively at the participating members' home center in the privacy of a secluded room. Informal interviews, on the other hand, occurred in almost every conceivable location, from early morning walks in the woods to afternoon restaurant meetings to midnight van trips enroute to a district recruitment center.

Former cult members' interview location ranged from their home or apartment to restaurants and late night diners in the Ann Arbor area. Parents of current or former members were interviewed in their homes or at various locations in and around the Detroit area.

All the interviews were arranged to meet best the convenience, needs, and time constraints of the study's participants. Consequently, the interview schedule varied from early morning to late evening sessions. Conditions for the interviews fluctuated between ideal (quiet, comfortable home) to poor (a lively restaurant). Nevertheless, the quality of the setting appeared to have little impact, positive or negative, upon the participants in the study. They were all receptive and willing to discuss any question or issue raised by the author.

The Pre-Interview Format (Formal)

Before permission was obtained for each interview, a series of steps was initiated by the author. These steps served as safeguards to assure that each subject understood completely the intent and requirements of the study.

Each potential participant was called on the telephone and given a brief overview of the study including the author's academic and professional credentials. If the potential subject expressed an interest in participating in the study, an appointment to meet was arranged at the subject's convenience. Before the interview was conducted, a lengthy explanation of the study's purpose and design was presented to each subject. A verbal script (see Appendix B) was read or summarized for each participant. The script included information regarding 1) the requirements established by the Human Subjects Review Committee of the School of Education of the University of Michigan, 2) the design of the study including

169

its intent, 3) the interview format style, and 4) the subject's responsibilities should he or she decide to contribute to the study. If at this point, the subject expressed a willingness to participate, he/she was given a Consent Form (see Appendix A) for review. The author then went through a verbal point by point explanation of the participant's rights as a subject in this study. Upon agreement with these safeguards, the subject was requested to sign and date the form. Permission to use a tape recorder was requested of each subject before the interview.

Formal Interview Format

In order to understand why some people commit themselves to an authoritarian religious movement that is far different from their original value system, one must obtain as complete a picture of each subject as possible. In the present study, an understanding of each subject's behavior change was viewed within the framework of the individual's personality structure. This included his perceptions, his values, his goals, his interests, his temperament, and his needs and drives. In addition, a thorough examination was made of the factors inherent within the situation that the individual occupied at strategic points in the conversion process.

All the subjects were interviewed extensively to elicit their impressions, attitudes, perceptions and factual data regarding a wide range of subject areas affecting their life (or their son's or daughter's life, as the case may be). The basic interview format was semi-structured in that it was conducted around a series of previously conceived open ended questions (see Appendices C, D, E). The structure was so designed as to maintain consistency among the subjects. The interviewer, nevertheless, maintained considerable freedom within the process. Questions, for example, were not necessarily asked each subject in the same order. To do so would have created confusion and a sense of discontinuity with the subject's previous answer. Further, the interviewer often branched off from the original question to explore ancillary areas of interest or underlying factors or relationships too elusive for the original straightforward question.

The subjects were given complete freedom of response in their answers. Ample time was allowed for each respondent to answer questions in a comfortable manner. There was no set time limitation placed on any interview. Participants were informed at the onset of the interview process that they could discontinue the interview whenever they liked. Interview times ranged from approximately 90 minutes to 4 1/2 hours. The author used a relaxed question method which allowed each participant an opportunity to talk about issues at the level that he/she felt most comfortable with. Subjects were never pressed to respond to questions nor asked to justify their answers beyond the level that they wished to discuss it. They were informed of their freedom to return to any previous statement which they wished to amplify, clarify, or change completely during the interview process. In addition, subjects were informed of a retrospective safeguard regarding their remarks. Any comments or questions within the interview session which caused them discomfort upon reflection would be eliminated from the transcriptions at their request.

Great care was taken to insure that each subject had a concise understanding of each question. Throughout the entire process, the author attempted to maintain a professional attitude of sympathetic neutrality toward the subjects, their ideas, their values and their lifestyles.

To insure that the rights of the participants in this study were in no way violated or compromised, several safeguards were established. Subjects were informed of their rights a minimum of three times before they were

171

allowed to participate in the study. Subjects
listened to a verbal rendition of their rights
during a pre-interview script presentation
containing an overview of the study. Subjects
read their rights on a Consent Form which was
provided each study participant. The author went
through a step-by-step explanation of the
subjects' rights before requesting their signed
permission on the Consent Form. All questions
that the subjects had about their rights were
immediately answered. Finally, subjects were
assured that any information or characteristics
that could in any way identify them as a subject
in this study would be eliminated from the final
publication.

Informal Interview Format

As a self-disclosed researcher and cult
outsider, I realized that my initial, formal
interview technique had severe limitations for
truly understanding the Moonie perspective and
lifestyle.

During the formal interview process
several members, encouraged by my open-minded
approach (and perhaps potential for conversion)
suggested I take a more active role in the
group's activities. Members from both the
Detroit and Ann Arbor centers began inviting me
to special events and informal dinners. Due to
the time and cost involved in commuting to the
Detroit center, I decided in the Fall of 1980
to limit the bulk of my efforts to the nearby
Ann Arbor Carp center. I began attending a
variety of group activities including
recruitment events, discussion sessions and
dinner rap sessions. In addition, I began
meeting some of the members outside the group's
center — at restaurants or occasionally at my
office. The format of these encounters remained
essentially unchanged, whether I was involved
with one person or several members
simultaneously. I would probe the member's
feelings, attitudes or insights about themselves
or issues involved in membership with the

172

movement. Frequently, the questions would parallel those asked members in the structured, tape recorded sessions. The informal interview process however, allowed for a more relaxed, less self-conscious atmosphere where cult members felt more confident expressing their feelings and views.

While I repeatedly emphasized the professional nature of my association with the cult, the members entertained the hope that I would eventually recognize the truth of their message and join them in the battle with Satan. They assigned me a spiritual parent whose responsibility it was to expose me to the cult's structured recruitment program. As a result, I was invited to attend a weekend workshop in Columbus, Ohio.

In all, I spent over 200 hours talking, listening, discussing and debating informally with Moonies. None of these conversations were recorded, nor are any comments from these informal sessions reported directly to the body of this study. Members were informed and understood that I might use the insights I garnered from these conversations to develop strategies or profiles of general Moonie characteristics. Informal sessions ranged from a few minutes to several hours. Impressions, insights and conversational anecdotes were transferred to a notebook, when it was convenient and used as a resource when writing this study.

EPILOGUE

Throughout the body of this study, I have endeavored to maintain an attitude of rigid objectivity toward my subjects, free of any personal commentary or judgement. A researcher, however, does not exist within an emotional void. A variety of feelings, opinions, sentiments and reactions toward the movement and its membership have doubtless crept their way into my memory constellation, forever altering my disinterested evaluation of the Moonie cult.

A question may logically be raised in reading this account as to my personal bias when observing or reporting my conclusions. In order to undertake a study of this nature it was necessary for me to get to know my subjects on a highly personal level. Over the course of my year long investigation I developed some intimate and intense personal relationships with several Unification Church members. I admit to the possibility that my feelings may have unknowingly spilled over into my analysis of the cult, in some ways coloring my final results. Early on in the study, however, I recognized my vulnerability to the issue of personal bias and I made every reasonable effort to separate my emotional reactions from my more scientific observations. I was determined to present my findings in a truthful and scientifically valid manner. I felt no responsibility to please or pacify any segment of my research population. Indeed, every major group mentioned in the study (Moonies, former members, cult experts and parent groups) came under some form of critical scrutiny.

My interaction with the cult membership was obviously not typical of the average recruit. Moonies were always aware of my researcher status and my presence surely altered their behavior in some ways. Interestingly, members chose to ask me a few personal questions during our association, preferring to be on the receiving end of most enquiries. The character of my interactions generally reflected a therapist-patient model where one party willingly reveals his intimate self while the other by agreement remains relatively anonymous. It was obvious from the first series of taped interviews where Moonies clamored to be recognized that they were flattered by my probing of their inner thoughts.

There was never a time when I came to believe or accept even remotely, the ideology or perspective of the Unification Church. I understood the Moonie reality which provided me a wealth of insights along with a healthy dose of empathy for their condition.

I, of course, was not aware of the possibility of conceiving an alternative reality until I was well into my personal interaction with the membership. As most other people, I assumed that the Moonies had developed some secret formula for turning college students' brains to mush. I was frankly both frightened and exhilarated by my early contacts with them. It was like mentally running across an ice covered lake; I felt secure but I knew that at any point the ice might crack and the lake would swallow me up. Even as I became familiar with the group I never completely dropped my guard or let my affection for certain members overrule my judgement. My accessible position dictated caution. I felt like the man who tested the first parachute; if my judgement was in error the fall could be disastrous. As a result I took certain precautions like signing a deprogramming request form (Appendix F) before embarking upon a weekend recruitment seminar. If they really did possess mind altering techniques I wanted a safety net to ensure a

176

pleasant landing. Neither did I take their
theology or philosophy at face value.   I
examined each piece of information like a wary
customer might who was purchasing expensive
jewels from a shifty looking street vender.   I
scrutinized every statement, held it up to the
light and probed it for errors. Moonies were
both amused and bewildered by my circumspection.
They frequently exhorted me to think with my
heart and give my over active brain an
occasional respite.

        Eventually they came to understand that I
was never going to accept their perspective even
though I understood it.   Out of the shadow of
this realization, a complicated and unique
relationship emerged with those who accepted it.
I became for some a sympathetic interpreter in
the outside world--a link that could bridge the
communication gap between two perspectives.
They learned to trust my judgement and realized
that I would never deceive them or hide my true
feelings. My relationship with the Moonies was
very special to me.   It was steeped in moments
of poignancy, humor, warmth and sadness. Very
few people have an opportunity to embrace two
realities simultaneously, and I will cherish the
memory of the experience.

        In the opening chapter of the study, I
posed several rhetorical questions regarding the
Unification Church and its membership.   I have
laboriously endeavored, throughout the body of
this research, to answer these questions in a
disciplined and intellectual fashion.   To
respond to each of these questions on an
emotional level would require an entirely new
dissertation. Nevertheless, I feel compelled to
provide some kind of emotional closure to the
study which will put the research in some
perspective. The following paragraphs are my
attempt to convey the jumbled mass of emotional
reactions I have toward my experience with the
Unification movement.

        If one were to take the sum of all the
questions which began this study and somehow
compress them into one meaningful problem

statement it would probably read, "Who are these people called the Moonies anyhow?" To get at my deepest feeling I need to take a somewhat circuitous route.

When friends or acquaintances first learn of my research, they invariably want to know what Moonies are really like. Conditioned for years by an anti-religious cult media blitz, they eagerly await the usual round of stories and folk tales about brainwashed zombies and bizarre candlelight religious rituals. They hunch forward in their chairs in anticipation of lurid details, prepared in advance to cluck with outraged indignation at cruel cult practices during the obligatory pauses in my narration for dramatic effect. When I reply (and honestly so) "that I never met a Moonie I didn't like" their faces generally register profound disappointment or worse, shocked concern--concern born out of the suspicion that I have been unknowingly recruited into the legion of unthinking Moonie automatons. Without horror stories, their interest and my credibility as a cult researcher quickly dissipate. It seems few people are seriously interested in hearing information about a cult that contradicts their deeply embedded stereotypes. To say something nice about a Moonie elicits a reaction I can only compare with complimenting a Nazi.

The truth about Moonies (at least as I observed it) is neither dramatic nor simple. Certainly the cult members I met were not the strange or alien creatures the media would have us believe. Rather they are, for the most part, the youthful products of a sanitized suburban environment, holding the same hopes, fears, illusions and dreams as most other middle class Americans.

In the Moonies, I often recognized myself at twenty, naive, energetic, idealistic and ever ready to shake a corrupt world by its very foundation. Certainly the Unification message is far from unique at its central core. The promise of world peace, love and community were the underpinnings of the message that wafted its

178

way through my generation of youthful idealists in the 60s on a wave of rock music and marijuana smoke. Moon merely needed to pick up the tattered shards of a dying dream and to wave the banner anew for another naive generation to claim as its own.

Moonies are young people who trust their hearts more than their heads--prisoners of either their inflated expectations or their passion for acceptance. Many members have a ferocious talent for self deception, locking themselves in a death grip of rationalizations when faced with overwhelming evidence that suggests they are wrong. But that is to be expected from individuals who embody the imagination, pride or desperation to believe that God has somehow plucked them from the anonymous mass of humankind to lead the world in a revolt against evil.

Mostly, however, when I take a long range reflective view of the Moonies I see the struggle of all mankind--the search for beauty, truth, self respect and meaning in an otherwise menacing environment. The Unification goal of worldwide salvation and happiness, after all, is the foundation upon which all religion rests. If the membership wishes to pursue these goals then I wish them well. Moonies truly believe (at least at the beginning) that they are serving mankind--for this I admire them.

APPENDICES

APPENDIX A

INFORMED CONSENT FORM

The research project to be conducted by Roger Dean, a student of The University of Michigan's School of Education, as a dissertation has been explained to me.

I understand that:

1) my participation is completely voluntary

2) all information is confidential and my identity will not be revealed

3) I am free to withdraw my consent and to discontinue my participation in the project at any time.

4) any questions I have about the project will be answered.

If I agree to participate I will:

On the basis of the above statements, I agree to participate in this project.

_____	_____
Participant's	Investigator's
Signature	Signature
	Roger Dean
_____	1310 Wisteria, #4633
Date	Ann Arbor, MI 48104
	(313) 995-4058

182

APPENDIX B

SCRIPT

My name is Roger Dean and I am a graduate student in the School of Education at The University of Michigan. I am currently at work on my doctoral dissertation, which is a study to determine the reasons why some people commit themselves to a religious movement that is so different from their original value and belief system. I would like to talk with you about your (past) (son's or daughter's) involvement in the Unification Church.

Before I explain the method and design of my study, I would like to reassure you that your comfort, consideration and feelings toward this topic are of great concern to me. It is important that you understand that the research of my study is in no way meant to judge, challenge or change you in regard to any of your beliefs, philosophies or lifestyles. I simply want your opinions, insights and any other information you may wish to give in regard to this area.

To insure that your rights as a participant in this study are in no way violated or compromised, my dissertation committee has established several safeguards that I would like to explain to you. If you would like additional information, clarification, or you do not fully understand any of the following points I am explaining to you please do not hesitate to ask questions.

183

First, this study is completely voluntary and you may decide to stop at any time you please during the study.

Second, you will have complete and unquestioned freedom to refuse to answer any question or questions in the study that make you feel uncomfortable for any reason.

Third, all your responses to the questions will be kept strictly confidential as will your identity as a participant in this study.

Fourth, any information or characteristics that could in any way identify you personally as a subject in my study will definitely be eliminated from the final publication of my dissertation.

Fifth, I would be happy to answer any questions you might have about any aspect of the study before, during or after our interview.

The design of the study itself is very simple. I would like to sit down with you on a face to face basis and discuss your (son's or daughter's) involvement as a member of the Unification Church. I have developed a number of open ended questions that I would like you to answer. These questions range from facts about yourself and your background to reasons why you made (or your son or daughter made) a commitment to the Unification Church. I may on occasion, branch off into some impromptu questions, brought on by some interesting point in your discussion. Therefore, all my interviews will not be totally identical. I would like to emphasize that you will be given complete freedom of response in your answers. I favor a very relaxed style of interviewing and you will certainly be given plenty of time to answer every question to your satisfaction. Should you want to return to a previous statement or question to expand on it or completely change your view after reflecting on it; that is perfectly acceptable. With your permission I will be using a tape recorder to make sure I

understand all of your statements. I will be
transcribing the tapes to a written interview
form and I may use some of your perceptions in
the final draft of my dissertation. There is no
set time limit on the interview or interviews.
We can start and stop whenever it is most
convenient for you. Likewise, we can hold the
interviews any place that you would feel most
comfortable discussing the topic.

If you have any questions that you would
like to ask me about the study, my background or
interest in the topic area I will be happy to
discuss it with you. Please feel free to think
about whether you want to participate in the
study. Be assured that if you do not want to
become involved in this study that there are no
negative implications.

Thank you.

APPENDIX C

OUTLINE OF INTERVIEW QUESTIONS:
CURRENT MEMBERS

Tell me about yourself (your interests, hobbies, accomplishments--whatever you would like me to know about you).

Could you describe a typical day in your life?

How did you first hear or learn about this group?

Why did you (or didn't you) find the group attractive?

What was your initial reaction to the group's goals and philosophy?

How long after your first introduction to the group did you decide to become an active member?

Was it difficult for you to commit yourself to the group and its ideals? Did you think about your decision for sometime before deciding to join?

Did you talk over the alternatives with other people before joining? Who? For how long?

How did individual family members react to your joining this group?

Would you say that your relationship with your family has changed as a result of your joining this group? How?

How would you characterize your current relationship with each member of your family?

Did you consider that most people, outside your group, feel somehow threatened by the group? Did this bother or upset you in any way?

Are there ever any occasions where you are somewhat hesitant to announce to others that you are a member of this group?

What is the most important thing to you about being a member of this group?

What is the most difficult thing for you about being a member of this group?

What would you say is the most satisfying thing about your life right now?

Do you feel that you have changed a great deal after you joined this group? In what ways?

Do you maintain close contacts with friends outside of this group?

How do you think people who knew you before you joined this group would describe you today?

Does it ever bother you when those outside your group, through gesture or verbally, belittle the goals and philosophy of your group?

Many people feel that you have been somehow °brainwashed' into joining this group. What do you think?

Why do you think so many people believe it is all right to attempt to deprogram members of your group?

What are your feelings about former members of your group who have undergone 'deprogramming' and now denounce the goals and philosophy of the group?

Do you believe it is possible for someone whom you like and respect to convince you that membership in your group is not in your best interest?

OUTLINE OF INTERVIEW QUESTIONS;
FORMER MEMBERS

Tell me about yourself (your interests, hobbies,
accomplishments--whatever you would like me to
know).

How did you first become involved with this
group? Tell me about your first contact.

Were you initially attracted to this group?
Why?

How would you characterize your life at this
point? (attraction stage)

What kind of things (activities, member
personality, group dynamics, etc.) made the
group attractive to you?

What was the group's (individual or total)
impression or reaction toward you at this point?

Were you aware that this group had any type of
image or reputation in the community?

How would you describe the group's recruitment
efforts?

Why were they successful in recruiting you, or
others?

How are new members attracted and brought into
the group? Is there a conscious, deliberate
process?

Would you say that the group used some
systematic methods to attract you to the group?
If so, could you elaborate on these methods or
techniques.

Does this group espouse a doctrine or philosophy? Could you give me a brief explanation of it?

How is the doctrine transmitted to new or potential members?

Were there ever any subtle or overt efforts to get potential members to join the group?

Did you experience any reservations about becoming a member of this group?

What made you decide to become an active member of the group?

Can you remember when you made the decision to join?

Was there some type of initiation or recognition ceremony when you joined?

What is the process involved in becoming an active member of this group?

Are many people rejected by the group who would like to become members? Why?

After becoming an active member, how did this alter your life?

Did your decision to join the group affect your relationship with your family? Friends?

Had you discussed your desire to join the group with anyone prior to your becoming an active member?

How would you characterize your responsibilities to the group (personal, social, work, etc)?

What was the reaction of those outside the group toward you as an individual and/or the group? How did you feel about this?

Were you ever afraid or hesitant to identify yourself as being a member of this group?

How did you and other group members cope with
the negative feedback you received from people
outside your group?

What was the best thing about being a member of
this group?

What was the worst thing about being a member of
this group?

Did you ever think of leaving the group? When?

How would you characterize yourself (attitudes,
emotional state, behavior, etc.) while you were
a member of this group?

What was the leadership hierarchy like?

How did someone become a leader in this group?
Did most people want to advance and become
leaders?

What were the advantages/disadvantages of
becoming a leader in this group?

What kinds of methods were employed to maintain
or keep members in the group?

What happened when someone left the group?

Did you ever feel physically or psychologically
threatened by the group? If yes, elaborate.

Describe a typical day in your life as a member.

Do you feel that members of this group are in
some way different from non-members? How?

Do you feel that the group significantly alters
a person once he becomes a member? In what
ways?

What made you decide to leave the group?

After leaving the group, did you have any
reservations or a desire to return?

How would you characterize your feelings after
leaving the group?

Do you feel that the group has had an impact on
you today? If so, how?

What are your views about deprogramming?

How would you characterize your feelings toward
the group today?

APPENDIX E

OUTLINE OF INTERVIEW QUESTIONS: PARENTS OF CURRENT/FORMER MEMBERS

When did you first learn that your son/daughter had joined the Moonies?

What were your son's/daughter's circumstances at the time he/she joined? (age, what doing at the time, etc.)

How would you characterize his/her life at this point? (just prior to conversion)

Why do you think he/she joined?

Did he/she ever talk over the decision to join the group with you? Another family member? A friend you are aware of?

Do you know how the group made their first contact with your son/daughter?

How long after their initial encounter did your son/daughter decide to become a member?

What was your initial reaction to learning that he/she had become a member?

Have you ever tried to dissuade your son/daughter from the decision to be a Moonie?

What method did you use?

Do you feel that your attitude toward the group had any effect on your son's/daughter's decision to remain in the Moonies?

How would you describe your son/daughter as a child? a teenager? immediately before becoming a Moonie?

Do you believe that your son/daughter had any particular characteristics that may have:

>1) made him attractive to the Moonies so that they would seek him out?

>2) may have made the group highly attractive to him/her?

Why do you feel individuals (other than your son/daughter) join the Moonies?

Before becoming a member, did your son/daughter ever talk to you about his goals or plans for the future? What did he/she want out of life?

Did you maintain contact with your son/daughter while he/she was a member? If not, why?

Did you notice any difference in your son/daughter after he/she become a Moonie? (emotionally, physically, etc.)

What is it like being the parent of a Moonie? (positive or negative)

Did you son's/daughter's membership affect your life in any way?

In raising your son/daughter would you make any significant changes in the method(s) you employed?

Do you have any advice for other parents whose son/daughter has joined the Moonies?

What is your reaction to deprogramming Moonies?

If your son/daughter is no longer a member have you noticed any lasting impressions of the group on his/her behavior, attitudes, or lifestyle?

APPENDIX F

    I, Roger Allen Dean, give my written
permission to be deprogramed in the event that I
join the Unification Church as a result of their
weekend indoctrination program.

_____

Witnessed the 27th of December 1980

_____

_____

_____

BIBLIOGRAPHY

BIBLIOGRAPHY

Aronson, Elliot. The Social Animal. 3rd ed.
San Francisco: W. H. Freeman and Co.,
1980.

Aronson, E., and Mills, J. The effect of
severity of initiation on liking for a
group. Journal of Abnormal and Social
Psychology, 1959, 59, 177-181.

Asch, S. E. Social Psychology. New York:
Prentice-Hall, 1952.

Asch, S. E. Studies of Independence and
Conformity: A minority of one against a
unanimous majority. Psychological
Monographs, 1956, 70, No. 9, Whole No.
416.

Atkinson, J. W. (Ed.) Motive in Fantasy, Action
and Society. Princeton: Van Nostrand,
1958.

Atkinson, J. W., and Feather, N. T. (Eds.) A
Theory of Achievement Motivation. New
York: John Wiley, 1966.

Back, K. W. Influence through social
communication. Journal of Abnormal and
Social Psychology, 1951, 46, 9-23.

Beck, Aaron T., and Young, Jefferey E. College
Blues. Psychology Today, 1978, 12, 80-
92.

Berger, P. L. Invitation to Sociology: a
humanistic perspective. Garden City:
Doubleday, 1963.

Blau, Peter M. _Bureaucracy in Modern Society_.
New York: Random House, 1965.

Boettcher, R. B. _Gifts of Deceit_, New York:
Hold Rinehart and Winston, 1980.

Boslooper, T. "The Character of Unification
Theology As A Modern Christian
Statement." Unification Seminary, New
York, 1978. (Mimeographed)

Byrne, D. _The Attraction Paradigm_. New York:
Academic Press, 1971.

Bryne, D., Landon, O. and Reeve, K. The effect
of physical attractiveness, sex, and
attitude similarity on interpersonal
attraction. _Journal of Personality_,
1968, _36_, 259-271.

Clark, J. G. Cults. _Journal of the American
Medical Association_, July 20, 1979, _242_,
No. 3, 279-281.

Clark, J. G. "The Manipulation of Madness."
Harvard Medical School at Massachusetts,
1908. (Mimeographed)

Coe, G. A. _The Spiritual Life_. Chicago: The
University of Chicago Press, 1900.

Conway, G. and Siegleman, J. _Snapping_. New
York: Lippincott, 1978.

Damrell, J. _Search for Identity: Youth,
Religion and Culture_. California: Sage
Publications, 1978.

Darly, J. M. and Darby, S. A. _Conformity and
Deviation_. New Jersey: General Learning
Press, 1973.

Divine Principle: Six Hour Lecture. New York:
The Holy Spirit Assoc. for the
Unification of World Christianity, 1977.

Erikson, E. H. _Young Man Luther_. New York: W.
W. Norton, 1958.

197

Erikson, E. H. Insight and Responsibility. New
     York: W. W. Norton, 1964.

Erikson, E. H. Identity, Youth and Crisis. New
     York: W. W. Norton, 1968.

Festinger, L., Schachter, S., and Back, K.
     Social Pressure in Informal Groups. New
     York: Harper, 1950.

Festinger, L., Riecken, H. W., and Schachter, S.
     When Prophecy Fails. Minneapolis: Univ.
     of Minnesota Press, 1956.

Festinger, L. A Theory of Cognitive Dissonance.
     Calif.: Stanford Univ. Press, 1957.

Festinger, L. and Carlsmith, J. M. Cognitive
     Consequences of Forced Compliance.
     Journal of Abnormal and Social
     Psychology, 1959, 58, 203-210.

Galanter, M., Rabkin, R., Rabkin, J., and
     Deutsch, A. The Moonies. A
     psychological study of conversion and
     membership in a contemporary religious
     sect. American Journal of Psychiatry,
     1979, 136, 165-169.

Garnier, M. A. Power and Ideological
     Conformity: A case study. American
     Journal of Sociology, 1973, 79, 343-363.

Gerth, H., and Mills, C. W. Max Weber: Essays
     in Sociology. New York: Rautledge and
     Kagan Paul, 1948.

Hitler, A. Mein Kamph. New York: Stackpole
     Sons, 1939.

Huston, T. Foundations of Interpersonal
     Attractions. New York: Academic Press,
     1974.

James, W. What is an emotion? Mind, 1884, 9.

James, W. _The Varieties of Religious Experience_. New York: The New American Library, 1929.

Kaplan, M. A. _Alienation and Identification_. New York: The Free Press, 1976.

Kim, Y. O. _Unification Theology_. New York: The Holy Spirit Assoc. for the Unification of World Christianity, 1980.

Knight, J. A. "Religious-Psychological Conflicts of the Adolescent." In _Adolescent-Contemporary Studies_, pp. 377-396. Edited by A. Winder and D. Angus. New York: American Book Co., 1968.

Liftan, R. _Thought Reform and the Psychology of Totalism_. New York: Norton Press, 1963.

Lofland, J. _Doomsday Cult_. New York: Irvington Press, 1977.

Meerloo, Joost A. M. _Rape of the Mind_. New York: Grosset and Dunlap, 1961.

Milgrim, S. Some Conditions of Obedience and Disobedience to Authority. _Human Relations_, 1965, 259-276.

Newcomb, T., and Flacks, R. _Deviant Subcultures on a College Campus_. Ann Arbor: University of Michigan Press, 1963.

Nock, A. D. _Conversion_. New York: Oxford Univ. Press, 1961.

Parsons, T. _The Social System_. Glencoe: The Free Press, 1951.

Patrick, T., and Dulack, T. _Let Our Children Go_. New York: E. P. Dutton and Co. Inc., 1976.

Reiss, A. Social organization and socialization: variations on a theme about generations. Mimeographed paper. Dept. of Sociology, Univ. of Mich., 1966.

Reisman, D. The Lonely Crowd. New Haven: Yale
    Univ. Press, 1950.

Rice, B. Honor Thy Father Moon. Psychology
    Today. 1976, 9, 36-47.

Rokeach, M. Beliefs, Attitudes and Values. San
    Francisco: Jossey-Bass, 1968.

Sargent, W. Battle For The Mind. New York:
    Doubleday and Co. Inc., 1957.

Schachter, S., and Singer, J. Cognitive, Social
    and Psysiological Determinants of
    Emotional State. Psychological Review,
    1962, 69, 379-399.

Speer, A. Inside the Third Reich: Memoirs.
    tr. Richard Winston and Clara Winston.
    New York: Macmillan, 1970.

Stinchcombe, A. L. Rebellion in a High School.
    Chicago: Quadrangle Books, 1964.

Stoner, C., and Parks, J. A. All Gods Children.
    Radner Penn.: Chilton Book Co., 1977.

Toffler, A. Future Shock. New York: Random
    House, 1970.

U.S. House of Representatives. Committee on
    International Relations. Investigation
    of Korean-American Relations. 95th
    cong., 2d. sess., 1978.

U.S. Senate. Information Meeting on The Cult
    Phenomenon In the United States. Chaired
    Senator Robert Dole. Washington, D.C.:
    Feb 5, 1979.

Walster, E. "Passionate Love: in Theories of
    Attraction and Love. pp. 201-216.
    Edited by B. I. Murstein. New York:
    Springer Publ., 1971.

Weber, Max. <u>Theory of Social and Economic Organization</u>. tr. A. M. Henderson and T. Parsons. Fairlawn: Oxford Univ. Press, 1947.

Willner, R. A. <u>Charismatic Political Leadership - A Theory</u>. New Jersey: Center of International Studies at Princeton, 1968.

Winder, A., and Angus, D. <u>Adolescence - Contemporary Studies</u>. New York: American Book Co., 1968.

Wrong, D. The oversocialized conception of man. <u>American Sociology Review</u>, 1961, <u>26</u>, 183-193.